Osprey Modelling • 36

Modelling the Messerschmitt Bf 109F and early G series

Brett Green

Consultant editor Robert Oehler • *Series editors* Marcus Cowper and Nikolai Bogdanovic

First published in 2007 by Osprey Publishing
Midland House, West Way, Botley, Oxford OX2 0PH, UK
443 Park Avenue South, New York, NY 10016, USA
E-mail: info@ospreypublishing.com

ISBN 978 1 84603 113 7

Page layout by Servis Filmsetting Ltd, Manchester, UK
Typeset in Monotype Gill Sans and ITC Stone Serif
Index by Alison Worthington
Originated by United Graphics Pte Ltd, Singapore
Printed and bound in China through Bookbuilders

07 08 09 10 11   10 9 8 7 6 5 4 3 2 1

A CIP catalogue record for this book is available from the British Library.

FOR A CATALOGUE OF ALL BOOKS PUBLISHED BY OSPREY MILITARY
AND AVIATION PLEASE CONTACT:

NORTH AMERICA
Osprey Direct, c/o Random House Distribution Center, 400 Hahn Road,
Westminster, MD 21157, USA
E-mail: info@ospreydirect.com

ALL OTHER REGIONS
Osprey Direct UK, P.O. Box 140, Wellingborough, Northants, NN8 2FA, UK
E-mail: info@ospreydirect.co.uk

Photographic credits

Unless otherwise indicated, the author took all the photographs
in this work.

Acknowledgements

In this latest Osprey Modelling title it is my pleasure to showcase
the modelling and painting talents of Chris Wauchop, Glen Porter,
Jamie Davies, Laurence Farrugia and Anthony Sheedy, plus the
authentic light and shade of Tom Tullis' profiles.

This book would not have been possible without the expertise
and assistance of a number of individuals who are specialists in
their fields. In particular I would like to thank John Beaman, Jerry
Crandall, Lynn Ritger and Steven Eisenman for their information,
advice and opinions over the years. Thanks also to Dr Charles E.
Metz and his encyclopedic reference collection.

I am very grateful to Jerry Campbell from Squadron, Dave
Klaus from Meteor Productions, David Hannant from Hannants,
Gaston Bernal from Aeromaster/Eagle Strike and Kevin
McLaughlin from Ultracast for their ongoing enthusiastic support.

And last but certainly not least, thanks to my wife Debbie and
our children, Charlotte and Sebastian, for their continuing
indulgence.

Contents

Introduction

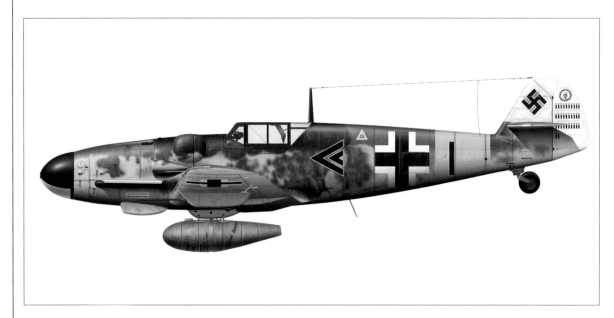

A Messerschmitt Bf 109G-6/R6, the mount of Hptm. Anton Hackl, *Gruppenkommandeur* of III./JG 11. The fin and rudder of this aircraft have been painted white as an additional identification measure.

The Messerschmitt Bf 109F represented a transformation compared to the squared-off lines of the Emil. This sleek hunter now featured a new large aerodynamic spinner, streamlined cowling and rounded wingtips. The Friedrich was arguably the most attractive of all the Messerschmitt Bf 109 variants.

The installation of the Daimler-Benz DB 605 A engine in the Messerschmitt Bf 109G increased power, but an upgrade in armament, armour and options resulted in a corresponding increase in weight. The once-nimble fighter was becoming overloaded as more missions were demanded of it. Even so, the Gustav remained the workhorse of the Luftwaffe, with more than 12,000 of the G-6 variant alone being produced.

This book will deal with modelling the Augsburg Eagle from the introduction of the Bf 109F through to the Bf 109G-6 and G-14, the last of the variants fitted with the Daimler-Benz DB 605 A engine.

Table 1: Bf 109F-1–G-14 production variants and characteristics

Designation and sub-types	Key identifying characteristics	Comments
Bf 109F-1	Improved aerodynamic shape compared to Bf 109E, including revised cowling, large streamlined spinner, redesigned wing with new split radiator flaps and landing flaps; rounded wingtips and unbraced horizontal stabilizers. Engine-mounted, centre-firing MG-FF cannon. Wing guns deleted. Daimler-Benz DB 601 N power plant with a larger metal three-bladed VDM propeller than the E series. New radio configuration required lower fuselage whip antenna.	The Bf 109F-1 was preceded by four prototypes and possibly a small Bf 109F-0 production series. Deliveries of the Bf 109F-1 commenced in Autumn 1940. Production totalled 208.

Bf 109F-2 F-2/B (Jabo) F-2/U1 (MG131 cowl guns) F-2/R5 (300-litre drop tank)	Centre-mounted MG-FF replaced with MG151/15 (15mm) cannon. External stiffener strips added to the tail across Frame 9 during production run. Circular wheel well opening introduced during production. External armoured windscreen glass fitted individually.	First major production variant of the Bf 109F. Deliveries began January 1941. Total production around 1,380.
Bf 109F-4 per F-2 plus F-4/Z with GM-1 F-4/Trop F-4/R1 (Gondola cannon armed) F-4/R2, R3, R4, R5 (recon variants)	Fitted with Daimler-Benz DB 601 E engine with improved performance on lower octane fuel. Centre-mounted gun replaced with MG151/20 (20mm) cannon. Larger diameter supercharger intake introduced during production. Internal tail strengthening introduced during production resulting in omission of tail stiffener straps.	Introduced into service in June 1941. Total production of 1,841
Bf 109G-1 Bf 109G-1/R6 (Gondola- mounted 20mm cannon)	Specialized high-altitude variant with pressurized cockpit. New air intake scoops on engine cowl. Revised cockpit armour to seal canopy. Welded canopy construction. Daimler-Benz 605 engine with new cooling scoops. Larger oil cooler. Relocated fuel filler hatch. Windscreen design revised, and cleaner tube installed. Broader propeller blades	Introduced into service June 1942. Total production 167.
Bf 109G-2 R1, R2, R3, R6, U1 and Trop	Per G-1 without pressurization equipment and associated fittings. Some fitted with the vertical head armour of the G-1. Ventilation scoops below windscreen, and rectangular ventilation flaps mid-fuselage (not all machines).	Introduced into service June 1942. Total production around 1,586.
Bf 109G-3	Per G-1, plus new features introduced on the G-4 (listed below).	Introduced into service March 1943. Total production 50.
Bf 109G-4 R1, R2, R3, R4, R6, R7, U1 and Trop	Per G-2. Fuselage antenna wire lead-in moved aft between Stations 7 and 8. Larger main wheels and non-retractable larger tail wheel, plus bulges on top of wings to accommodate wider wheels introduced during production. 'Galland Panzer' canopy armour in late-production machines.	Introduced into service November 1942. Total production around 1,242.
Bf 109G-5	Specialized high-altitude variant with pressurized cockpit and associated fittings. Otherwise similar to G-6 below.	Introduced into service December 1943. Total production of 475
Bf 109G-6 Sub-types per earlier variants plus U2, G-6/N, G-6/Y Bf 109G-6/AS will be dealt with in a future volume	Per G-4. Cowl machine guns replaced with MG131s, requiring large bulges to accommodate belt chutes. Redesigned gun troughs. New inspection hatch on rear fuselage. The following improvements were introduced at various stages during production. DF loop, shorter antenna mast/no antenna mast (attached direct to fuselage), Galland Panzer canopy armour, Erla Haube clear-vision hood, tall fin and rudder (different patterns and Flettner/trim tab configurations), Morane mast for FuG 16ZY	Introduced into service February 1943. Total production of more than 12,000.
Bf 109G-8	Specialized photo reconnaissance variant based on the Bf 109G-6	Introduced into service November 1943. Total production greater than 900.
Bf 109G-12	Two-seater trainer based on reconditioned Bf 109G-2, G-3, G-4 and G-6 airframes. Usually unarmed. Typically fitted with 300-litre under- fuselage drop tank.	Introduced into service around March 1944. Total production less than 500
Bf 109G-14 Bf 109G-14/AS will be dealt with in a future volume	Per G-6	Introduced into service July 1944. Total production of around 5,500.

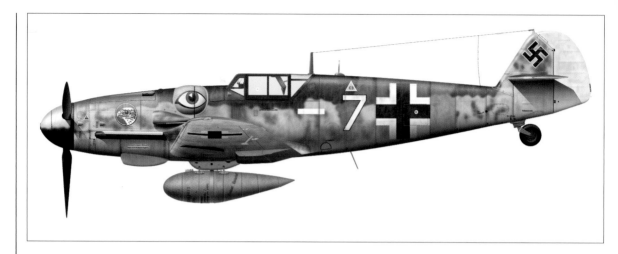

'White 7', a Messerschmitt Bf 109G-6 of JG 51. Of interest is the large eye on the gun bulge, the JG 51 emblem on the cowling, the overpainted fuselage band and the unusual position of the II Gruppe bar ahead of the aircraft number.

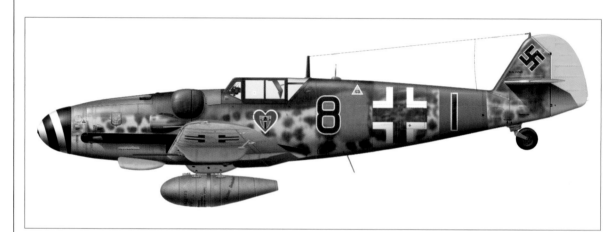

ABOVE Black 8, W.Nr. 26048, a Messerschmitt Bf 109G-6/R6 of 8./JG 54. This colourful aircraft was flown by Offz. Gunther Sahl at Luneburg in Germany during the spring of 1944

BELOW Messerschmitt Bf 109G-14, White 21 of II/JG 52. This aircraft wears typical late-war southern theatre markings on the nose and the rudder.

Hidden details of the Messerschmitt Bf 109G-6

This chapter contains a number of images of some Messerschmitt Bf 109G-6 parts not normally visible in wartime photos or museums.

LEFT This is the oil cooler on the bottom of the cowl of Messerschmitt Bf 109G-6 W.Nr. 163824 at the Australian War Memorial in Canberra. Although the airframe is a G-6, this appears to be the deeper oil cooler housing normally associated with the Bf 109G-10 and K-4.

BELOW, LEFT This style of oil cooler is noticeably deeper than the G-6 version.

BELOW, RIGHT The shell-ejector chutes for the 12.7mm cowl guns can be seen behind the big oil cooler housing. It is interesting to note that the panel surrounding the ejector ports is wooden.

Here is the supercharger intake on the same aircraft. Note the prominent weld seam along the centre line.

Here is the gun cowl cover and the lower forward cowl cover. Note the wide difference in colours.

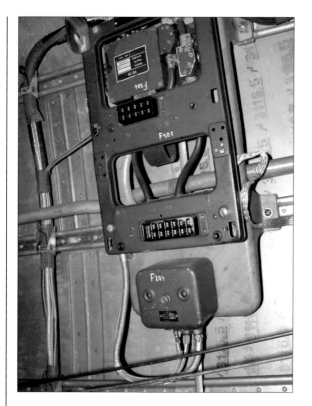

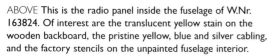

ABOVE This is the radio panel inside the fuselage of W.Nr. 163824. Of interest are the translucent yellow stain on the wooden backboard, the pristine yellow, blue and silver cabling, and the factory stencils on the unpainted fuselage interior.

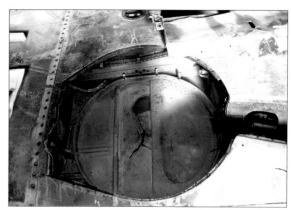

ABOVE RIGHT This is the panel for the FuG 16ZS radio direction finder inside the rear fuselage. The same yellow stain has been employed for the wooden backboard.

RIGHT This is the wheel well from a Messerschmitt Bf 109G-6 undergoing restoration in Australia. Note the pressed metal bulge in the roof of the wheel well to accommodate the wide tyre.

A different view of the same wheel well reveals lightening holes in one end, and in the gear leg covers closer to the camera.

Panels stripped from the bottom of the wing reveal internal structural detail and RLM 02 Grey paint in immaculate condition.

Bf 109F and Bf 109G in plastic

General summary

As one of the most famous fighter aircraft in history, it is not surprising that the Messerschmitt Bf 109 is well represented in plastic.

In the small scale of 1/144, Eduard released a Bf 109F and G kit in the 1990s, followed by Sweet's excellent Messerschmitt Bf 109F-2/4 in recent years. The Sweet Friedrich belies its tiny size with crisply recessed panel lines and a very accurate shape. This kit set new standards for 1/144 scale.

In 1/72 scale, Hasegawa updated its old Messerschmitt Bf 109G-6 kit with a completely new release around 1988. This model featured recessed panel lines and improved accuracy compared to the original Hasegawa kit. The separate rear fuselage assembly hinted at the tall-tail Bf 109G-14 that followed a few years later. For many years, Hasegawa's Gustavs were the best 1/72-scale injection-moulded Bf 109s available, but they do suffer from a few problems. The spinner is too small in diameter, which means that the nose is a little narrow. The canopy and windscreen look undersized, and the shape of the tail surfaces on the G-14 kit do not look quite right. Typical of 1/72-scale kits of this era, the cockpit is basic too.

Academy released 1/72-scale Bf 109G-6 and G-14 kits a few years later. These models shared very similar parts breakdown and all the same dimensional weaknesses as Hasegawa's kits. In addition to the inherited errors, Academy's horizontal tailplanes seem to be mounted too low on the empennage.

In late 2004, Fine Molds of Japan launched their brand new range of 1/72-scale Bf 109F and G kits. These surpass the Hasegawa kits in every respect. They are accurate, well detailed and cleverly engineered. They even include some basic engine block details under separate cowlings. We will examine the Fine Molds 1/72-scale Messerschmitt Bf 109G-6 in more detail later.

Over the years, there have been a large number of Bf 109F and G releases in 1/48 scale. Some of these are no longer readily obtainable, such as the Fujimi family of Bf 109Gs. Others soldier on after decades, including the Arii/Otaki Gustav, which may still be found under the Airfix label today. In addition, the

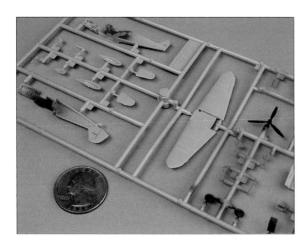

Japanese company Sweet released the first in a series of 1/144-scale Messerschmitt Bf 109s in 2003. The parts breakdown is simple but detail and accuracy are very good.

Sweet's 1/144-scale Bf 109s fit together very well too. Some filler may be required on the gun cowl insert to blend it with the nose.

9

Airfix 1/48-scale Messerschmitt Bf 109F, originally released in 1978, currently remains in their catalogue. Despite some inevitable evidence of ageing – sink marks, soft detail and some raised panel lines – it remains a decent kit worthy of consideration.

In 1991, Hasegawa released their first 1/48-scale Messerschmitt Bf 109F kit. More than 15 years later, we continue to see new Bf 109F and G releases derived from these original sprues. Hasegawa treated Messerschmitt fans to their 1/32-scale Gustav series from 2001 onward.

If you are planning to build a Messerschmitt Bf 109F or G in 1/32 scale, Hasegawa should be your first choice. Hasegawa has set the milestone for Messerschmitt modelling excellence. We will examine Hasegawa's 1/48- and 1/32-scale kits in detail over the coming pages.

Hobbycraft released a large variety of 1/48-scale Bf 109F and G kits in the 1990s, which have been re-released by Academy. These more recent boxings offer superior decals to Hobbycraft, but otherwise display the shortcomings of the original releases including poorly shaped detail parts, small canopy and windscreen, and indifferently detailed cockpits.

Hasegawa's 1/48-scale Bf 109F and G-2 kits

During its brief but spectacular tenure in the late 1980s, Japanese model manufacturer Trimaster single-handedly lifted the standard of 1/48-scale WWII model aircraft.

Hasegawa responded to the challenge with a spate of new releases including a Messerschmitt Bf 109E series with photo-etched parts, followed by the Bf 109F-2 in 1991.

Hasegawa's Bf 109F-2 featured crisp engraved panel lines, accurate outline and some really useful options including positionable canopy, separate flaps and slats. Cockpit detail was a little sparse but represented a good basis for detailing. Accuracy problems were limited to a slightly bulbous spinner and incorrectly shaped drop-tank mount.

The initial F-2 spawned a long-lived series including an F-4, F-4/Trop, F-4 Winter and G-2. All these kits shared the same basic set of fuselage and wing sprues with different parts supplied for oil cooler housings, supercharger intakes, propeller blades, tail wheels and canopies. Most of these models provided plenty of spare parts once the model had been finished.

These kits were generally easy to build, but the fuselage assembly proved a little tricky due to flimsy fuselage halves and separate engine cowlings.

This is Hasegawa's 1/48-scale Messerschmitt Bf 109F-2, the first in their series of F and G variants. At the time of their release in 1992, these were the best Bf 109s available in any scale.

Hasegawa's 1/48-scale Bf 109G-6 and G-14 kits

When Hasegawa produced the great workhorse of the Bf 109 series, the G-6, they took a fresh approach. Two sprues, including the wing, were from the existing 109F/G series. Three, including the fuselage, were new. Surface detail was as crisp and delicate as the earlier kits, but the new fuselage halves were more robustly engineered with a smaller gun trough insert for the top of the engine cowling.

There are a few small ejector-pin marks on the gear doors, the tail wheel and the main wheel hubs. Any other ejector marks are on the unseen inner surface of parts.

Cowl bulges are separate pieces. Options for both main styles of starboard bulges are provided (i.e. with and without the small scoop and bulge). We are also offered the option of a tropical air filter.

The bulges on top of the wings to accommodate the wider wheels of the late G series are also separate pieces. These require locating holes in the wings that are visible through the open wheel wells.

The interior is identical to the previous offerings except for the instrument panel. A breathtaking range of detail sets for Bf l09s is available to improve this area, including products from MDC, Cutting Edge, Eagle Editions, CMK, Eduard and more. The kit also features separate flaps and slats.

Ordnance in the initial release was limited to a centre-line drop tank and under-wing MG151 20mm gun packs, but other specialized options became available in later releases.

Accuracy is generally good, but there is around 2mm missing from the fuselage between the front of the windscreen and the rear of the engine cowling.

Hasegawa's 1/48-scale Bf 109G-14

Hasegawa's 1/48-scale Bf 109G-14 is every bit as nice as the initial G-6 release. The main differences are a new sprue for a G-14 fuselage featuring the tall tail, an alternative pressed gun trough for the forward cowl (although the insert version issued with the G-6 is still included as an option – G-14s were seen with either), and an Erla Haube clear-vision canopy. The framed canopy is also included as some G-14s still used this style.

Cutting Edge decals were used for Hans 'Assi' Hahn's markings. Hahn was *Kommodore* of JG 2 on the Channel Front during 1941.

Hasegawa's 1/48-scale Bf 109s make a good basis for super-detailing. This is Hasegawa's Messerschmitt Bf 109G-2/Trop kit, built by Jamie Davies.

The model has been super-detailed with a number of accessories, including CMK's comprehensive engine set.

The Daimler-Benz DB 601 engine is supplied by CMK in resin with photo-etched details. The set also includes thin resin cowl covers. Jamie has further enhanced the engine bay with fine wire.

The two soldiers in Jamie's diorama have been adapted from 1/48-scale British Infantry and Afrika Korps figures. There has been a recent growth in 1/48-scale figures and accessories.

Hasegawa's 1/48-scale Messerschmitt Bf 109G-6 and G-14 kits featured an all-new fuselage, clear-vision canopy plus a number of revised parts.

This is Chris Wauchop's 1/48-scale Messerschmitt Bf 109G-14, finished as a participant in Operation *Bodenplatte*. This aircraft was shot down on 1 January 1945.

Chris enhanced the clear-vision Erla Haube hood with a restraining cable and a canopy release lever. The bulge for the relocated battery compartment has been added behind the pilot too.

Lower surface details are well done on Hasegawa's kit, with crisp panel lines and the option of a 300-litre drop tank.

Decals were sourced from Aeromaster sheet number 48-222.

Over the years, Hasegawa has released more than 20 variations on the Bf 109G-6/14 theme, with an impressive selection of Luftwaffe and foreign air force markings.

Hasegawa's 1/32-scale Messerschmitt Bf 109G-6

Hasegawa's first 1/32-scale Gustav release was the Bf 109G-6 in 2001. Early rumours suggested that this model was a scaled-up version of their 1/48 Bf 109G-6. This was not the case – the 1/32-scale kit was totally new. In fact, with this release, Hasegawa addressed many of the criticisms of the smaller kit.

Hasegawa's 1/32-scale Messerschmitt Bf 109G-6 is packed in a large sturdy box. The sprues contain 107 parts in grey styrene, 11 parts in clear and four polythene caps. Hasegawa persist in packaging all the grey sprues in a single bag. As a result, some of the larger parts were scuffed on arrival. Clear parts are packed separately with the decals. Nine parts are marked 'not for use'.

Although the model is labelled a Bf 109G-6, most of the parts required to build a G-5 variant are also present. Options include two styles of upper cowl panel (pressed-metal gun troughs and insert gun troughs); alternate starboard side gun bulge with oil bubble remover housing; windscreen with air scoop or flare port; Galland Panzer or standard steel head armour; 2 x 20mm cannon gondolas; 300-litre drop tank; plus positionable slats and flaps. A seated pilot figure is also supplied.

Surface detail is superb. Panel lines are crisply engraved, hinges are beautifully depicted and the fabric surfaces are worthy of special mention. The subtle fabric tape is topped with delicate stitching detail. Rivet detail is selective, but adds an air of authenticity where it is present on the lower wing, radiator housing and tailplanes.

Fuselage and cockpit

The fuselage is supplied in four main parts. The tail is separate aft of fuselage panel 7. This simplifies tooling for the tall-tail versions of the Gustav. A stout rectangular tongue moulded onto the fuselage section of the tail ensures a positive join with the main fuselage halves.

Hasegawa released their 1/32-scale Messerschmitt Bf 109G-6 in 2001. This is a well-detailed kit that includes many useful options. The model wears the colourful markings of 9./JG 54.

This model was built using Cutting Edge's resin cockpit set. This cockpit is simple to install but adds significant detail to the Gustav's front office. Markings were sourced from EagleCals decal sheet No. 41.

Chris Wauchop built his 1/32-scale Hasegawa Bf 109G-6 as a late version fitted with the Erla Haube clear-vision hood. This model was built before the release of the Hasegawa G-14 kit, so Falcon's 1/32-scale vacform Erla Haube hood was used.

The scoops on the forward cowl are moulded open. The two scoops on each cowl side are moulded staggered. There are a number of possible configurations for these scoops on the full-size Bf 109G-6, ranging from a noticeable horizontal stagger to perfectly in line, so check reference photos and relocate if required.

The port fuselage side includes two pips below the cockpit. These are the mounts for an umbrella that was sometimes used in tropical environs. Although these were not installed on most non-tropical Gustavs, check your references carefully because they may have occasionally been present.

Also, in common with the 1/48-scale kit, two small hatches must be filled and sanded on the starboard side fuselage. These were filler hatches for the GM1 and MW50 injection system employed on later variants (although they are applicable for an early G-14 with framed hood and standard tail).

The interior of the supercharger intake is free of locator pins, giving a clear view through to the moulded supercharger fan detail on the fuselage side.

The exhaust manifolds and deflectors assemble in the same way as the 1/48-scale kit. The exhaust stacks are not hollow and neither are the machine-gun barrels. Drilling these out in 1/32 scale does not present any great challenges.

A simple horseshoe oil cooler is provided for the front of the fuselage. This locks in place with a twist.

The cockpit is quite conventional. The seat pan is supplied as a separate part. The seat back was not usually installed in these later 109s, and the kit reflects this configuration. Some detail is moulded onto the sidewalls, and other features including the quadrants are separate parts. The instrument panel is a single plastic part with raised detail. A decal is supplied as an alternative to painting. One very nice touch is the inclusion of a door for the small stowage hatch behind the pilot's head. Not only does this depict an oft-ignored feature, but it also helps to hide a tricky join line.

Perhaps the most significant engineering feature in this kit is the mid-lower fuselage panel. The panel represents the centre section of the wing, and it includes a stout, 'H'-section wing spar. This ensures perfect dihedral and a good fit at the wing root.

Wings and tailplanes

The wings feature positionable flaps and slats. The flaps and slats have locating tabs to improve strength and ensure even alignment. This is another improvement over the 1/48-scale kit.

Chris's model was finished in the striking markings of Luftwaffe ace Erich Hartmann. Decals are from EagleCals.

The wheel wells display some nice rivet and structural detail. They even have the appropriate indent to correspond with the bump on top of the wing. The bump is still a separate part though, and two locating holes protrude into the wheel well. These should be filled and sanded before the wing halves are joined.

The glass insulator for the Morane mast is provided as a clear part. This is nice attention to detail. The perspex covers for the navigation lights are clear parts too.

Bits and pieces

The centre section of the canopy has a ridge on the starboard lower edge. This is to help locate the canopy in the open position – another difficult task on the 1/48-scale kit. The landing gear is nicely detailed, even including moulded-on brake lines.

The profiles of the ETC rack. drop tank and gondolas look good.

The oil cooler housing on the real aircraft had a small supporting strut in the centre of the forward air intake. The kit oil cooler housing has a locating hole in the correct spot, but the strut itself is not supplied. Stretched sprue or fine rod will do the job.

Instructions are typical of Hasegawa. Construction is called out in 14 steps by the use of exploded-view diagrams. Gunze paints are quoted throughout the instructions.

This kit has been released under several boxings with a good selection of markings.

Dimensions and profile

Comparison with Tom Seay's and John Beaman's drawings suggest that the fuselage is the correct length to within 1mm. The miniscule discrepancy seems to be directly in front of the windscreen. Wing dimensions are spot on.

One other area of concern with the 1/48-scale kit was the shape of the spinner. The spinner in this 1/32-scale kit is noticeably better.

Hasegawa subsequently released a number of additional Messerschmitt Bf 109 variants in 1/32 scale, including a Bf 109G-4 and a G-14. This is the Bf 109G-14 kit built by Anthony Sheedy.

Hasegawa's 1/32-scale Messerschmitt Bf 109G-14 kit

Hasegawa's second 1/32-scale Gustav was the tall-tail Messerschmitt Bf 109G-14, released in mid-2002.

This variant was produced with several different styles of rudder. Variables included the construction material (fabric skinned or plywood); the presence of trim tabs and Flettner tab and the shape of the rudder base. Hasegawa has supplied a single option with fairly typical fabric-covered rudder with the squared-off bottom, two external Flettner tabs and one trim tab. A separate part is supplied as the trim tab actuator. The fabric stitching details match the rest of the kit.

The Erla Haube clear-vision hood is also produced to a very high standard.

Interestingly, the kit does not include the bulged battery box cover behind the pilot's head (a feature of all MW50-equipped G-14s), nor the option of a tall-tail wheel (admittedly, an irregular feature of the G-14). Neither are the standard tail or framed canopy included in the box, limiting the options for building the entire range of G-14s.

Hasegawa's 1/32-scale Messerschmitt Bf 109G-4/Trop kit

Hasegawa's most recent Gustav release is the Bf 109G-4/Trop. This same kit also appeared in a Revell box.

Hasegawa's Bf 109G-4 is more than a simple change of box and decals, but not much more. The only differences are a new top cowl with the correct MG troughs, new machine-gun barrels, a blanking plate for the lower fuselage (replacing the shell-ejector panel on the G-6/G-14 kits) and a tropical filter. The new top cowl looks good.

The model still includes the gondola cannon. These are appropriate as there was a G-4 'gunboat'. It may also be built as a standard G-4 if the tropical filter is omitted and the umbrella mounting pips are removed from the fuselage sides.

The model perfectly captures the distinctive lines of the Messerschmitt Bf 109G.

Anthony's model has been enhanced with the Aires resin cockpit along with a replacement spinner, oil cooler and drop tank from Eagle Parts. The canopy has been detailed with a restraining wire and spring, and the bulge typical of all MW50-equipped Bf 109s (accommodating the relocated battery) has been added to the pilot's stowage door. Anthony has also added rivet detail to the entire airframe, drilled out the exhausts and fabricated weld beads and brake lines.

However, for purists, this kit does not address several Bf 109G-4 characteristics. The instructions are also a little misleading in a few areas:

- Revell supply the same rear fuselage/fin as in the G-6 kit. Most Bf 109G-4s had an open tail wheel well, not faired over as in the G-6. A little cutting will be required here, and some thought about how to mount the tail wheel strut. Also, the style of cover for the tail wheel strut was different to that of the G-6. Just to complicate matters more, this cover was not always fitted.
- The tail wheel supplied is the large style appropriate for later G-4s. This wheel was fixed in the 'down' position, as it was too big to fit in the tail wheel well. Earlier G-4s were fitted with a smaller, retractable tail wheel (not supplied in this kit).
- The oval inspection hatch between fuselage stations 8 and 9 (behind the jacking hole) on the port side should be filled and sanded.
- The join line between the top cowl and the cowl sides is not a panel line. This will need to be carefully filled and sanded smooth.
- The Morane mast was not fitted to the G-4. Glue the isolator/base (part R3) in place under the wing, then fill and sand smooth.
- Don't use the Galland Panzer pilot's armour (parts A26, R5 and R6). This was not fitted to the G-4. Use the solid plate armour (part B16) either by itself or with the curved top extension (part B15). Check your references to see which style is appropriate for your subject.
- The kit-supplied main wheels are the correct width for most G-4s, but the plain hub style was not typical. The 'spoked' style is on virtually every photo of a G-4 that I have seen. Also, early G-4s did not have the wing *Beule* (bump) and were fitted with the same narrow wheels as the G-2. If you are building an early G-4 you are in luck – True Details produce a resin set of narrow-spoked wheels.

Fortunately, most of these issues are very easily addressed.

Trumpeter's 1/24-scale Bf 109G kits

In 2003, Trumpeter simultaneously released two variants of the Messerschmitt Bf 109G in 1/24 scale – the Bf 109G-2 and the Bf 109G-6, early version. These were followed in 2004 by a late version with the tall tail and Erla Haube hood.

ABOVE Hasegawa's Messerschmitt Bf 109G-14 kit includes the distinctive tall tail and the clear-vision Erla Haube hood. Note that, in addition to the fabric-covered rudder supplied in the kit, several other styles of rudder were also fitted to tall-tail Gustavs.

BELOW In 2003, Chinese model company Trumpeter released their 1/24-scale Messerschmitt Bf 109G-6, early version and a Bf 109G-2. This is the Trumpeter Bf 109G-2 kit, built by Laurence Farrugia.

Trumpeter's kit includes an engine that may be displayed under open cowls. All the basic structures are supplied, but some extra work is worth the effort in this scale.

Cockpit detail is acceptable but, likewise, the front office will benefit from additional detailing. A photo-etched harness is supplied in the kit.

The subject of this examination, the Bf 109G-6 kit, comprises 272 injection-moulded parts in grey plastic and clear styrene (including a second set of fuselage halves in clear plastic), vinyl tyres, a small bag of metal rods, a photo-etched fret with hinges for control surfaces and an acetate sheet with printed instruments, as well as Aeromaster Decals for two aircraft.

The parts are well moulded with crisply engraved panel lines, supplemented with subtle rows of recessed rivets. Although surface detail is a very subjective issue, I think that this surface detail is quite acceptable in 1/24 scale.

Fabric surface detail on the control surfaces is represented by simple raised ridges. The texture is more restrained than earlier efforts but will still benefit from a few swipes of the sanding stick.

Two sets of canopies are supplied. The transparent parts are thin and clear, but the opening section of each canopy is scuffed on the inside. This looks like some sort of mould flaw and will require a few minutes of polishing to correct the problem. The clear instrument panel is also very thin, and should look good overlaying the acetate instruments after a coat of paint.

All control surfaces, including slats and flaps, are workable thanks to the inclusion of hinges made from etched metal and steel rod. The undercarriage gear is sprung, but (mercifully) does not retract. The small louvres at the front of the radiators are supplied as separate parts and may be positioned open or closed. Actuator struts are also included. Cowl scoops are moulded onto the kit nose and are open at the front.

The cockpit is acceptable, but is not as good as Hasegawa's 1/32-scale kits. Some detail is moulded onto the sidewalls, with separate parts added to this area. A harness is not included.

Trumpeter supplies a basic engine that will benefit from additional detailing. Individual exhaust stacks are split down the centre line and hollowed at the end. The cowl machine-gun barrels are also hollowed out, saving the modeller some extra work.

Optional parts include two 20mm under-wing gondolas. Indeed, the kit even incorporates the circular ammunition drum for each gondola inside the wing. This level of detail extends to the lower fuselage shell-ejection panel, which includes open holes for the chutes.

A 300-litre drop tank, alternate style wheel hubs, a DF loop and short antenna mast are also included. Although not mentioned in the instructions or parts list, a tall rudder is on Sprue H. A little scratch building would be required to the tip of the kit fin to fit this rudder, but it would not be too hard to make this modification if desired.

The Galland Panzer pilot's armour is moulded as a single solid grey plastic part. This style of pilot's head armour is more common to later G-6 aircraft, and in any case should be fitted with armoured glass. You'll need to cut out the centre of the plastic part and insert some clear plastic if you want to use the Galland Panzer. Furthermore, the more common early style solid-steel canopy armour is not included in the kit. Fortunately, this will be simple enough to cut from plastic sheet. Similarly, the longer antenna mast more frequently seen on early G-6s is not included but can be easily cut from scrap plastic.

All control surfaces, cowl flaps, radiator intake, oil cooler flaps and engine cowlings are supplied separately and may be positioned to taste. Tyres are vinyl.

Trumpeter's 1/24-scale Gustav is quite accurate in outline and impressively large when built.

Detail on the canopy parts includes handgrips on the windscreen, the canopy release lever and slide-window knobs.

The kit decals represent a vast improvement over earlier releases in Trumpeter 1/24-scale kits. They are produced by Aeromaster and cover two interesting subjects. Both have appeared on Aeromaster sheets in other scales. The decals are thin and in perfect register.

Accuracy

I compared the fuselage of Trumpeter's 1/24-scale Messerschmitt Bf 109G-6 with plans in my book, *Augsburg's Last Eagles*. The plans were scaled up from 1/48 to 1/24. Dimensions matched almost perfectly.

The depth and shape of the fuselage components looked excellent but there was a tiny discrepancy around the rear fuselage. Heading toward the tail, the fuselage is angled slightly upward compared to the drawings. At the mid-fuselage, the kit part is a little more than 1mm deeper than indicated on the drawing. Minor dimensions look good, even in tricky areas like the space between the front of the windscreen and the back of the engine cowl.

The wings also compare very closely to plans, this time scaled up from the Aero Detail book on the Bf 109G.

Laurence hand painted the distinctive emblem for 9./JG 54. Indeed, most of the markings, including the Yellow 3 and *Gruppe* 'squiggle' were painted by hand with the assistance of homemade stencils.

Table 2: Messerschmitt Bf 109F and G kits in 1/144, 1/72, 1/48, 1/32 and 1/24 scale

	Brand	Item Number	Description	Comments
1/144 scale				
	Eduard	4405	Messerschmitt Bf 109F	
1/72 scale	Sweet	14114	Messerschmitt Bf 109F-4	Two kits in each box
	A Model	72125	Messerschmitt Bf 109F-4	Future release
	A Model	72036	Messerschmitt Bf 109G-2	Future release
	A Model	72132	Messerschmitt Bf 109F-4/6	Future release
	Academy	1670	Messerschmitt Bf 109G	
	Academy	1653	Messerschmitt Bf 109G-14	
	Airfix	1072	Messerschmitt Bf 109G-6	
	Fine Molds	FL-01	Messerschmitt Bf 109F-2	
	Fine Molds	FL-02	Messerschmitt Bf 109F-4	
	Fine Molds	FL-05	Messerschmitt Bf 109F-4/Trop	
	Fine Molds	FL-06	Messerschmitt Bf 109G-2	
	Fine Molds	FL-07	Messerschmitt Bf 109G-4	
	Fine Molds	FL-08	Messerschmitt Bf 109G-4	
	Italeri	53	Messerschmitt Bf 109F-2/4	
	Italeri	72	Mistel 1 Ju 88A4 & Bf 109F	Includes Ju 88 & Bf 109
	Italeri	63	Messerschmitt Bf 109G-6	
1/48 scale	Smer	860	Messerschmitt Bf 109G-6	
	Academy	1682	Messerschmitt Bf 109G-14	Ex-Hobbycraft
	Academy	2146	Messerschmitt Bf 109G-6	Ex-Hobbycraft
	Airfix	4101	Messerschmitt Bf 109F	
	Hasegawa	J-38	Messerschmitt Bf 109F	Hans Assi Hahn
	Hasegawa	JT-26	Messerschmitt Bf 109F-2	
	Hasegawa	J-27	Messerschmitt Bf 109G-6	'Hungarian Air Force'
	Hasegawa	J-48	Messerschmitt Bf 109G-14	
	Hasegawa	J-29	Messerschmitt Bf 109G-2	
1/32 scale	Hasegawa	J-47	Messerschmitt Bf 109G-6	
	Hasegawa	8148	Messerschmitt Bf 109G-4	Reggia Aeronautica
	Hasegawa	9559	Messerschmitt Bf 109G-4	Italian Air Force
	Hasegawa	ST-17	Messerschmitt Bf 109G-6	
1/24 scale	Hasegawa	ST-18	Messerschmitt Bf 109G-14	
	Trumpeter	2406	Messerschmitt Bf 109G-2	
	Trumpeter	2407	Messerschmitt Bf 109G-6	Early version
	Trumpeter	2408	Messerschmitt Bf 109G-6	With tall tail and Erla Haube hood

Mediterranean Messerschmitt

Subject:	*Messerschmitt Bf 109G-6*
Modeller:	*Construction, painting and markings by Glen Porter*
Skill level:	*Moderate*
Base Kit:	*Fine Molds Bf 109G-6*
Scale:	*1/72*
Additional detailing sets used:	*R6 cannon gondolas from Academy's Bf 109G-6*
Paints:	*Model Master enamels*
Markings:	*Kit decals plus some markings from Academy's Bf 109G-6*

Fine Molds' 1/72-scale Messerschmitt Bf 109F and G kits

Summary

Pros

- Crisp, appropriate and restrained surface details
- Separate radiator flaps
- Excellent fit
- High level of detail for this scale
- High quality decals
- Accurate

Cons

- One-piece canopy
- Fixed main flaps and slats
- Shallow cockpit sidewall detail

Fine Molds' 1/72-scale Bf 109 family in the box

Until Fine Molds came along with their excellent 1/72-scale F and G series of late model 109s, we had no worthwhile Bf 109Fs at all and only two decent Bf 109G kits, from Hasegawa and Academy, which still left a lot to be desired.

Although the new Fine Molds' Bf 109 kits are not perfect, they are very good and are not likely to be bettered for a long while. Fine Molds has also recently released a G-10 and a K-4.

Fine Molds' 1/72-scale Messerschmitt Bf 109G-6 is a magic little kit. You can actually build this kit as a G-4, G-5 or a G-6 if you can supply your own markings. Fine Molds supplies a host of options. These include alternate cowlings, oil cooler housings, wheels, tailplane, propeller and gun deck.

The only criticisms of the kit are shallow cockpit sidewall detail and the decal camouflage, which I think is too dark.

Construction

Construction started with the cockpit. The sidewalls from Hawkeye Designs' excellent resin cockpit were added to the rest of the Fine Molds' cockpit parts. Apart from the shallow sidewalls, Fine Molds' cockpit parts are very good indeed. All cockpit components were painted and detailed, both resin and plastic, before they were glued into the fuselage halves. Eduard pre-painted 'Color Etch' lap belts were also glued on before the fuselage was closed.

The canopy was tacked on and covered with Humbrol Liquid Maskol to form a mask for the cockpit from. The one-piece canopy was later removed before being cut into three parts.

Because the Fine Molds kits provide some detail on a basic engine block, the model was originally going to be built with the starboard cowling open to show some of the Daimler-Benz power plant. However, in the interests of speedy construction, this idea was eventually abandoned so the engine cowlings were glued shut.

Neither Fine Molds nor any other manufacturer in this scale offer the option of dropped landing flaps. The split flaps are on both upper and lower halves but the main flaps are on the upper half of the wing only. This makes life a little easier as there are only three sections to be cut off each wing. Simply cut each flap from the trailing edge with a razor saw and along the panel line with a sharp scalpel. The flaps can be reattached in the up position for painting and removed again later for finishing. My model was destined to be a cannon boat

but the Fine Molds kit (No. FL8) does not supply the under-wing gondolas. I had to obtain these parts from the Academy G-6 kit. These, along with the drop-tank mount, exhausts, air intake and tailplanes were glued on but all other small items were left off till after painting. The rest of the build was straightforward and fit was perfect. No filler of any kind was required.

Fine Molds' 1/72-scale Messerschmitt Bf 109 G-6, finished in the markings of the *Gruppenkommandeur* of I./JG 27.

Painting and markings

The model was painted with Model Master enamels after pre-shading with black and Tamiya Flat Green enamel was sprayed on to the rear fuselage and masked with Tamiya tape. Wheel wells were given a coat of RLM 02 and then filled in with Maskol before the first camouflage colour of RLM 76 Light Blue was applied over all lower surfaces and fuselage sides. RLM 75 Grey Violet was then sprayed freehand on the upper surface. Camouflage masking was applied over the RLM 75 on the wings and the spine before applying RLM 74 Grey Green. After all the masks were removed, the fuselage sides were sprayed with a mottle of RLM 74 and RLM 75. At this point, I sprayed the lower nose yellow. The flaps were now removed and reattached in the lowered position. The whole model was given a gloss coat of Tamiya Acrylic clear gloss in preparation for decals.

Most of the decals came from the kit. Here I encountered my first problem. The fuselage crosses came from the Academy G-6 kit. I have used many Academy decals before and had no trouble but these would not settle into the recessed panel lines no matter what I used. In the end I had to use a scalpel on them and was not very happy with the results. The black chevrons were then masked and painted.

The reason for using acrylic gloss, apart from giving the decals something to cling too, was that it dries very fast and enamel washes can be applied without disturbing the camouflage paint underneath. This was demonstrated in no uncertain terms, as I had forgotten to coat the chevrons with gloss and when I started using an enamel wash on the lower surfaces I promptly wiped them off. Not a major problem and a lesson well learned.

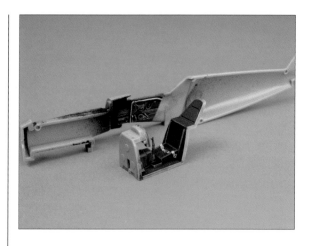

Fine Molds' cockpit is accurate and fairly complete, but sidewall detail is somewhat shallow. Resin sidewalls from the 1/72-scale Hawkeye Designs' cockpit set were therefore combined with the kit parts.

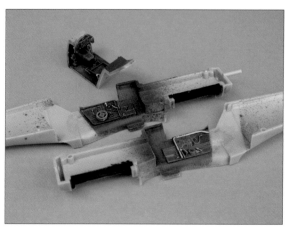

The cockpit interior has been painted with Model Master enamels. The harness was sourced from Eduard's pre-painted Color-Etch set.

Construction was straightforward and fit was excellent. Some basic detail is moulded onto the engine block, but it was decided to close the cowl on this occasion.

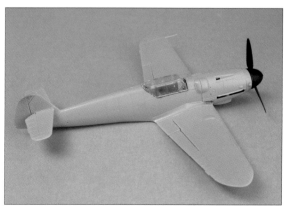

The flaps are not supplied as separate parts. Prior to assembly of the wings, the flaps were carefully cut away, ready to be repositioned on the finished model. The flaps have been temporarily tacked on for this photo.

Two different washes were used for the panel detail, both mixed at a ratio of four parts of thinners to one part of enamel paint. For the underside, I used Tamiya XF-63 German Grey and on the darker surfaces Flat Black. The wash was applied roughly along the panel lines and allowed to dry for about 30 minutes. Using a soft long-haired brush, I coated the surface with clean thinners. This took the unwanted wash off the raised areas leaving it in the ruts only. Care must be taken to mop the excess dirty thinners off the model. The same wash can be used to make oil and fuel stains, gunpowder marks and the streaky part of exhaust stains. If you are not happy with the results, you can simply wipe it off with clean thinners and start again.

After all the washes were dry and the model could be handled, paint chips were added around heavy wear areas such as the wing roots, engine cowlings, cockpit entry sill and regularly removed panels. This was done with a very fine brush and Tamiya Light Sea Grey enamel. When this was first finished, it looked too stark and overdone but after the model was dulled down it became less noticeable.

The model was painted with Model Master enamels after pre-shading with black. Tamiya Flat Green enamel was sprayed on to the rear fuselage and masked with Tamiya tape.

The canopy was glued in place before painting and masked with Humbrol's Liquid Maskol. This latex coat can be peeled off when painting is complete.

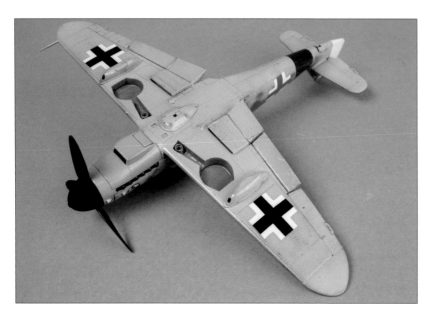

This Fine Molds kit does not include the under-wing cannon gondolas. These parts were sourced from Academy's Bf 109G-6 kit.

Fine Molds' kit decals were used for most of the markings, but the fuselage crosses and the black chevrons were sourced from the Academy Bf 109G-6.

Model Master Dullcote was sprayed over the model as the final flat finish. I initially applied a light, dusting coat and let it dry for about 15 to 20 minutes. This gave the two following heavier main coats something to grip on and avoided the Dullcote cracking and letting the gloss show through.

The canopy was now carefully removed and the glue was cleaned off both the canopy bottom and cockpit sill. I used a razor saw to cut the canopy into three pieces so the cockpit could be displayed open. It is a slow job and you have to check often that you are cutting straight. Once all three surfaces have a deep groove in them you can progress a bit faster. After separation, each component was cleaned up with a fine file and a sharp new scalpel.

The gunsight was painted and fitted, as were the two Eduard pre-coloured shoulder harnesses. The front and rear sections of the canopy were also glued on but the centre section was left until last. All the small protrusions that would have been easily broken off during handling were now fitted. The last job was fitting the opening canopy section. A small bead of white glue was run along the starboard side of the cockpit sill with a toothpick and the canopy carefully placed on in the open position. While the glue set the canopy was supported in the open position with a short length of Tamiya tape.

The model was now finished. Would I do anything differently next time? Yes, I put too much gloss coat on before decaling, which partially obscured some of the panel detail. I was also not careful enough cleaning up the cockpit cavity in the fuselage resulting in some problems fitting the canopy and lastly, I missed the wavy demarcation on the leading edge of the wings.

The Fine Molds kits are the best 1/72-scale late-model Bf 109s on the market and, although a small amount of cleanup is required, they are superbly detailed and result in a model that really captures the sit and look of the Messerschmitt Bf 109.

ABOVE The Academy decals proved to be uncooperative, failing to settle into panel lines until sliced with a sharp scalpel blade.

BELOW Fine Molds' family of Messerschmitt Bf 109s are without question the best injection-moulded 1/72-scale Friedrichs and Gustavs available today.

Friedrich in white

Subject:	Messerschmitt Bf 109F-2
Modeller:	Construction, painting and markings by Brett Green
Skill Level:	Moderate
Base Kit:	Airfix Bf 109G
Scale:	1/48
Additional detailing sets used:	Scrap plastic; brass rod; fuse wire
Paints:	Gunze acrylics using a Testor Aztek A470 airbrush
Markings:	Cutting Edge Decals sheet CED48243

Airfix's 1/48-scale Messerschmitt Bf 109F

Summary

Pros

- Reasonable surface details (combination of raised and recessed)
- Accurate
- Reasonable level of cockpit detail
- Simple parts breakdown and construction
- Available inexpensively

Cons

- One-piece canopy (undersized in E-3 kit)
- No option for dropped slats or flaps
- Surpassed in most respects by latest mouldings from Hasegawa

Introduction

Old is not necessarily bad. I am not just trying to make myself feel better as the years go by. I also try to apply this philosophy to my evaluation of plastic model kits.

There is little doubt that Hasegawa offers the best option for building a 1/48-scale Messerschmitt Bf 109F. Even so, there are other possibilities. Buried deep in my model collection was a 1/48-scale Airfix Bf 109F. Although theoretically superseded by Hasegawa, this 1978 release is very accurate in outline, has a beautifully clear canopy and a reasonably detailed cockpit. Surface features are a peculiar mix of recessed panel lines on the wings (with raised rivets below), and raised panel lines and hatches on the fuselage. Some aspects are simplified, including exhausts moulded onto the lower engine cowl, but there is something about the Airfix kit that authentically conveys the streamlined profile of this sleek fighter.

Construction

In contrast to the high-tech, super-detailed approach generally adopted today, I decided to revisit a gentler age. I would build this kit only using materials that were available at the Airfix kit's date of release in 1978.

The first DIY task was to separate the leading edge slats. The engraved lines for the slats were deepened with a scriber on the top and bottom wing halves to prepare for their removal. Without the option of after-market slats, I took care not to damage the plastic during preparation and final cutting out. The top and bottom halves of each slat were glued together, and the resulting gaps in the leading edge of the wing were filled with plastic card.

The next area crying out for attention was the gun troughs. The shape is good – I think that they are better than Hasegawa's – but they are shallow and the moulded-in gun muzzles are unconvincing. A hole for a new gun barrel was opened up with a drill before each trough was deepened with rolled-up coarse sandpaper.

Airfix's instructions would have you assemble the fuselage halves then add the cowls. This could lead to gaps and steps between the cowl halves and the forward fuselage. Instead, I attached each cowl half to its respective fuselage half prior to assembly. This allows perfect alignment with the fuselage at the vertical cowling panel lines. In fact, this method swaps the alignment problems on the fuselage sides for several gaps at the top of the nose. These gaps, however, are very easy to identify and eliminate once the fuselage halves are joined.

Before they are joined, however, it would be wise to deal with the various sink marks present on the fuselage halves, While I was filling and sanding, I also scribed a few of the filler and inspection hatches on the fuselage sides. I did not bother to scribe the vertical panel lines though. The inside mating edges of the spine were lightly bevelled with a sanding stick before assembly. This resulted in a recessed panel line along the spine when the fuselage halves were joined.

The Airfix cockpit looks bland in the box, but the deep sidewall detail responds very well to careful painting and weathering. The only modification to the kit parts was cutting off the back of the seat, and thinning the edges of the seat pan. I also formed a set of harness straps from lead foil (raided from a bottle of wine) and buckles from fine electrical wire. This jumble of straps will be the focus of attention through the closed canopy.

One area requiring some preventative attention prior to final construction is the fuselage wing root area. Test fitting suggested that the wings would not sit flush at the wing roots, so the plastic inside the wing root area was ground away.

With this excess material dispatched, the wings fitted perfectly without gaps or steps.

Smaller details were now added, including the supercharger intake, horizontal tail surfaces and the poorly shaped ETC rack. I did make a half-hearted attempt at reshaping the back of the rack, but ideally it should be replaced. The engine cowling hinge line and a weld line along the centre of the supercharger intake were fabricated from fine stretched sprue.

The Airfix 1/48-scale Messerschmitt Bf 109F may be old, but it is still quite a respectable kit. This model has been built using only materials that would have been available at the time of its release in 1978.

Painting and markings

My Friedrich was destined to wear a winter finish. The first step was a white primer coat, but this had nothing to do with the final camouflage. This aircraft featured prominent yellow Eastern Front markings. Yellow is notoriously difficult to spray with solid coverage, so the white undercoat helps to obtain a nice, solid coat of colour. I also chose to use Tamiya's Camel Yellow lacquer due to its fast-drying and robust qualities. This paint comes in a spray can but I decanted it into a jar to spray from my Aztek A470 airbrush.

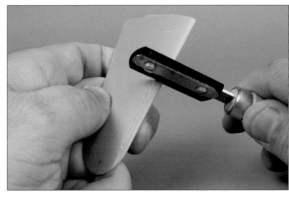

Messerschmitt Bf 109s are often seen parked with dropped slats. The engraved lines for the slats were deepened on the top and bottom halves of the wings prior to assembly.

A razor saw was used to slice a fine line at each end of the slats. A sharp knife along the length of the slat dispensed a neat finish to the job.

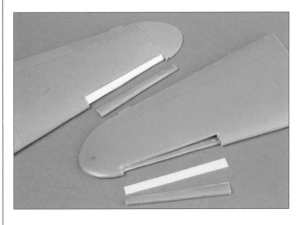

The top and bottom halves of each slat were glued together. A strip of plastic was measured, cut to width and glued to the front of the wing as backing for the open slats.

Gun trough detail is shallow and soft. The holes for the machine gun muzzles were opened with a twist drill. The troughs themselves were deepened using coarse sandpaper.

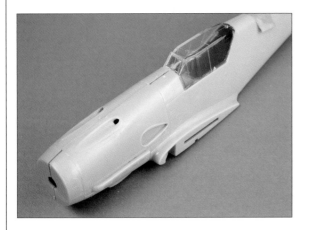

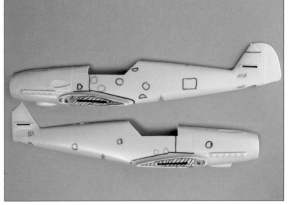

Airfix supplies separate engine cowlings, but their fit is problematic. I found it easier to glue each cowling to its respective fuselage half before assembling the fuselage. This results in a clean, step-free join on the fuselage halves. The resulting gaps on the top of the fuselage are easy to fill later.

A combination of old moulds and deep detail inside the fuselage has resulted in some sink marks. The green marker indicates these. The black lines are hatches and panels to be scribed. The cross-hatched area indicated inside the wing root will be ground away to improve the fit of the wings.

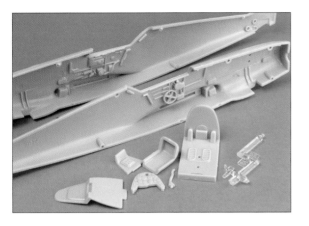

The Airfix cockpit comprises only seven parts, and is underwhelming prior to painting. However, it looks good with a minimum of effort.

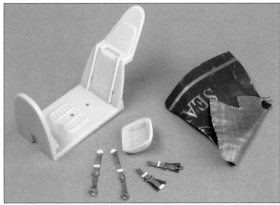

No aftermarket items were used, just strip styrene for seat rails on the rear bulkhead, and harness straps from lead foil. Buckles and anchor points were added using fine wire and scrap plastic. The seat back was cut off and the top edges of the seat pan were thinned with a hobby knife and sandpaper.

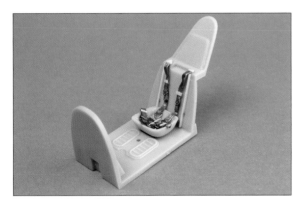

The homemade harness fills the space nicely. This harness will be the focus of attention through the closed canopy.

The deep sidewall detail responds very well to careful painting. All cockpit parts were first given a coat of Tamiya XF-1 Flat Black, followed by XF-63 German Grey. Details such as the harness straps, buckles and instruments were picked out with a fine brush.

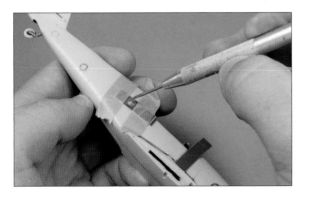

Circular filler hatches were scribed with the aid of Dymo tape templates. Circles were punched out of self-adhesive Dymo tape to create these customized scribing masks.

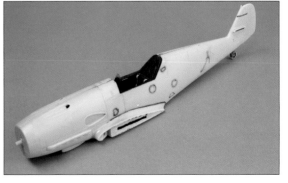

The fuselage takes shape. The vertical fuselage panel lines were not rescribed. Note that some plastic has been ground away inside the wing root. This will improve the join between the fuselage and the wings.

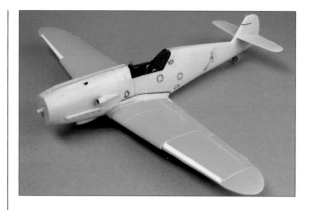

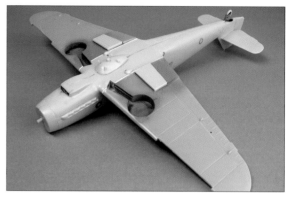

With this preparation, and after additional test fitting, the wings and tailplanes fit perfectly. The wings were temporarily tacked in place while dihedral was checked, then permanently bonded with liquid cement along the upper and lower wing roots.

The ETC rack is poorly shaped. The shape of the rear was modified, but it should really be replaced. A thin strip of plastic was glued along the bottom wing root join.

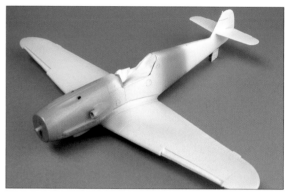

Painting was prefaced with a coat of Tamiya's Fine Surface Primer sprayed straight from the can. This white primer reveals any slip-ups, and also acts as a useful base for the yellow cowl and lower wingtips.

Tamiya's Camel Yellow was decanted from the spray can into an Aztek A470 airbrush. Tamiya's acrylic lacquers are tough and fast drying, especially welcome for colours as temperamental as yellow.

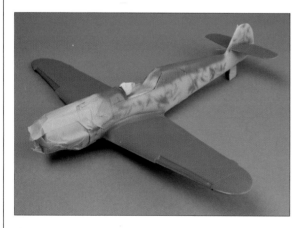

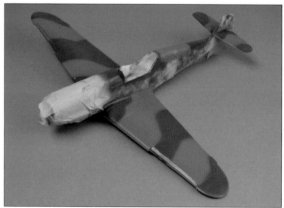

The yellow theatre markings were masked with Tamiya tape in preparation for camouflage colours. Although this subject was covered in a white winter coat, the base camouflage will add authenticity to the final result.

Gunze Sangyo acrylic RLM 74 Grey Green and RLM 75 were sprayed freehand onto the model. I was not too concerned about the authenticity of the pattern as it would be mostly obscured.

The white camouflage was sprayed carefully, being built up gradually using stripes and squiggles. The white paint was applied more thinly at leading and trailing edges.

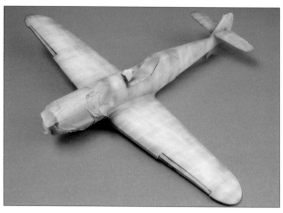

The overall effect is a slightly worn winter finish with a hint of the Luftwaffe day-fighter camouflage showing.

The yellow theatre markings offer striking contrast to the winter white camouflage. Here, the model has received an overall coat of Future floor polish as a gloss coat prior to the application of decals.

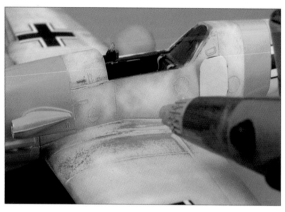

The paint job received some touch-ups and more attention in detail areas such as wing walks.

Markings were sourced from Cutting Edge Decals sheet CED48243. I especially liked the red devil's head emblem of JG 54's 9.Staffel.

Additional weathering was applied very sparingly to avoid overpowering the pale finish. The wing root area on the port wing was carefully rubbed back to reveal the camouflage colours beneath. Control surface hinge lines were subtly highlighted too.

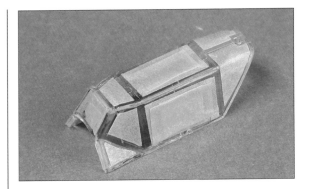

The kit canopy is a little thick but it is nice and clear. It was masked with Tamiya tape prior to painting.

Airfix's wheels are reasonably well detailed but have an open hub. The hub was covered with a circle and a bolt head punched from scrap styrene.

All subassemblies were brought together for final assembly. Note that the aerial mast and wire have already been installed even before the canopy has been attached to the fuselage.

Isolators were added to the aerial wire from small blobs of Kristal Klear, then painted light grey and black.

With the yellow paint dry and the theatre markings masked, I sprayed a basic camouflage scheme on the airframe, including the upper surface colours of RLM 74 Grey Green and RLM 75 Grey Violet. Hints of this original camouflage will show through the winter white, so this step is important. Even so, I did not spend too much time ensuring an accurate camouflage pattern or mottle – a suggestion of the scheme is enough.

Patience is the key when building up a winter whitewash finish. I started by spraying fine white lines and streaks on the wings and the fuselage. I was careful to vary the thickness of coverage, treating leading and trailing edges especially lightly. A number of random patches were also left relatively free of the white finish, especially the area where the fuselage markings would be applied.

I was pleased with the stark contrast between the yellow theatre markings and the white paint. The airframe received a coat of Future floor polish as a gloss coat prior to the addition of markings, which were sourced from Cutting Edge Decals sheet CED48243.

Once the decals were in place, round two of the winter whitewash commenced. This was a more focused application of very fine streaks and mottles, especially around the aircraft number, *Gruppe* bar and *Balkenkreuze*. I was trying to create the impression that these markings had been masked and sprayed around at the beginning of winter.

Additional weathering comprised very subtle highlighting of selected panel lines and control surface hinge lines with a thin mix of flat black and red brown, some rubbing back of the winter finish at the wing roots, and some further wear and tear in the same area with the tip of a silver pencil. The exhaust stains were sprayed onto the fuselage sides using the same brown/black mix that was used to highlight the panel lines. A few streaks and stains were brush-painted under filler hatches with heavily thinned acrylic black paint.

Finishing touches included adding hub detail to the main wheels using scrap plastic and a punch and die, masking and painting the one-piece canopy (which fitted beautifully, by the way), adding hydraulic lines to the gear legs from fine wire, and attaching a nylon antenna line to the aerial mast. The undercarriage doors were left off, as was common practice in winter to avoid the build-up of mud and slush. The wheels were also lightly dusted with Tamiya's white weathering pastels to suggest fresh snow.

The airframe received its final coat of Polly Scale Flat and the remaining items were assembled for a very different looking Friedrich.

The model was posed against a suitably wintry scene. The cardboard base has been sprinkled with baking soda, while the background is a photo of an authentic ex-Luftwaffe hangar in Germany.

ABOVE The gear doors were removed from many Messerschmitt Bf 109s in winter to avoid a build-up of slush and mud.

BELOW The Airfix 1/48-scale Messerschmitt Bf 109F stands the test of time as an attractive, if somewhat simple, rendition of this streamlined fighter.

A Finnish Gustav

Subject:	Messerschmitt Bf 109G-2
Modeller:	Construction, painting and markings by Brett Green
Skill level:	Master
Base kit:	Hasegawa Bf 109G-4 and G-6
Scale:	1/32
Additional detailing sets used:	MDC cockpit; MDC tail wheel; MDC 1/32-scale riveting tool; Aires main wheels; Aires wheel wells; Eduard Color-Etch harness; plastic strip, wire and scrap pieces
Paints:	Gunze and Tamiya acrylics using a Testor Aztek A470 airbrush
Markings:	MDC decal sheet D32007, 'Messerschmitt Me 109 G-2 Ilmavoimat 1943–44'

Construction

Sometimes a modelling project gets off to a bad start: this was one of those times.

My original plan was to backdate Hasegawa's excellent 1/32-scale Messerschmitt Bf 109G-6 to a G-2 using a number of parts from Aires' resin Bf 109F conversion. The first step was to add some surface detail to the model using MDC's rivet-making tool. While applying the rivets, I managed to punch the sharp tool straight through the thin resin and quite deeply into the side of my index finger. It might have been possible to fix the shattered resin but I thought I would take a different tack, using the gun deck from the Hasegawa/Revell Bf 109G-4 instead.

Once I had dressed my wound and continued riveting, I managed to crack the plastic on the rear of the kit fuselage. Clearly I was applying too much pressure! This time I was able to repair the damage and carried on without further incident. Adding rivets is undoubtedly a time-consuming and tedious task but I think it is worth the effort, especially in this large scale. I used a different technique this time though. Instead of using the photo-etched guide, I drew pencil lines onto the fuselage and wings, then used these as the sole guide for applying the rivets.

The cockpit was the next area to be addressed. Hasegawa's kit cockpit is not bad, but there are some marvellous multimedia replacements available. One of these is from MDC. MDC's 1/32-scale Messerschmitt Bf 109G-2 cockpit provides 19 perfectly cast and stunningly detailed parts in grey resin, plus photo-etched parts and decals. Cockpit detail moulded to the interior of the kit fuselage was removed, and the general area was thinned with a Dremel motor tool. The backs of the resin cockpit sidewalls were thinned too. It is well worth spending a little time with this preparation as the sidewalls will fit much more neatly beneath the cockpit sills, creating a more authentic impression and improving the later fit of the instrument panel.

All this detail responds well to careful painting. The sidewalls were glued to the interior of the fuselage and the cockpit tub parts were assembled before receiving a base coat of Tamiya XF-1 Flat Black paint. This was followed by Tamiya XF-63 German Grey sprayed in several light coats at a slightly downward angle. This technique preserves a trace of black paint in natural shadow areas. Tamiya XF-1 Flat Black was mixed with Tamiya XF-64 Red

Hasegawa 1/32-scale Messerschmitt Bf 109G family

Summary

Pros
- Accurate outlines
- Good level of detail
- Good fit
- Crisply recessed panel lines
- Separate flaps and slats
- Thin, clear canopies
- Useful options (drop tank, cannon gondolas, alternate gun decks and canopy armour etc.)

Cons
- A few sink marks

Germany exported the Messerschmitt Bf 109 to a number of Axis allies. This Bf 109G-2 saw service with the Finnish Ilmavoimat (Air Force) in May 1944.

Brown, which was thinned and sprayed in fine streaks and a few random mottles on the sidewalls, seat and rear bulkhead. The final weathering step was a selective wash of thinned raw umber. The oil paint was applied along the edge of boxes and structural detail using a fine brush. When applied subtly, this oil wash represents grime quite well. The cockpit detail of switches, handles, seat cushion, harness straps, buckles, instrument bezels, electrical wiring, hoses and the oxygen regulator were all picked out with acrylic paint and a fine brush.

MDC and Reheat stencil decals were applied to a number of structures on the cockpit sidewalls and the cannon breech cover. These decals look very effective in this large scale.

Although the MDC harness was very nice, I decided to substitute it with the Eduard Color-Etch pre-painted harness.

Another area worthy of attention is the wheel wells. To their credit, Hasegawa has moulded some structural features to the roof of the wheel wells, but the sidewalls and leg bays are fairly bare. Aires recently released a Bf 109G wheel well detail set comprising four resin parts. However, this set does not address the visible locating holes in the top of the wheel wells. These were first covered with plastic card, and then the moulded-on wheel well detail was carefully removed from the bottom wing halves with a Dremel motor tool and a pair of side cutters. The Aires wheel wells looked good when glued in place, with their depiction of canvas dust covers and lightening holes.

The fuselage halves and the wings were now assembled. Although the instructions suggest that the rear fuselage halves should be joined before attaching the tail to the assembled mid-fuselage, I recommend that each fuselage half should be assembled first – i.e. join the left fuselage and left rear fuselage; then the right fuselage and the right rear fuselage. Align the parts carefully and allow them to set before joining the two completed fuselage halves.

I also tried a different assembly technique for the wings. First, I had to reduce the height of the wing spar centre sections to clear the thicker resin cockpit floor. Next, instead of gluing the lower wing centre section to the fuselage, I built up a full-span wing comprising the lower centre section plus the left and right wing before the entire assembly was offered to the fuselage. This resulted in a perfect, gap-free fit when the wing was eventually mated to the fuselage. Dihedral looked a little flat though, so I encouraged another couple of degrees by stretching Tamiya tape from wingtip to wingtip until the glue dried.

The gun deck from the Bf 109G-4 kit fits quite well but leaves a prominent seam line along the bottom join on both sides. This was dealt with using Milliput two-part epoxy putty. First, the immediate area surrounding the seam was masked, and then the putty was mixed and trowelled on with my favourite putty tool – an old staple remover. The putty was smoothed with a damp fingertip then the masking tape was removed. The putty was blended again to eliminate the small ridge formed against the tape. After the putty had set overnight, it was sanded and polished, eliminating the seam altogether. Panel detail was restored, and surface details were carefully added to the gun deck and the remainder of the cowl using MDC's riveting tool.

The gun troughs on Hasegawa's G-4 are not entirely convincing. I think they look too flat – not like separate, drop-in pressings. The edges of the gun troughs

An astounding range of accessories is available for Hasegawa's excellent 1/32-scale Messerschmitt Bf 109 kits. Here is but a small selection, some of which will be used on this model.

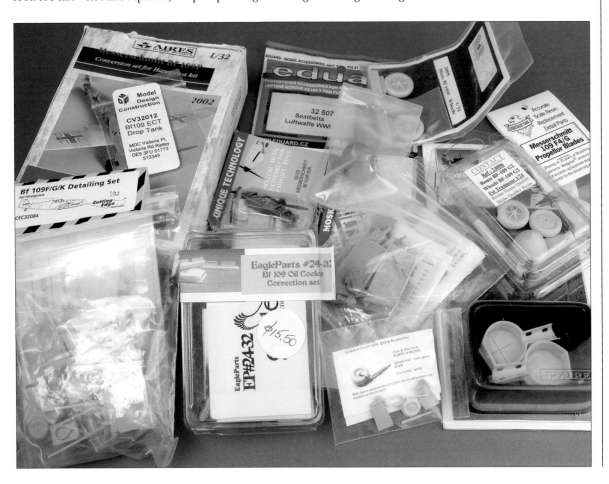

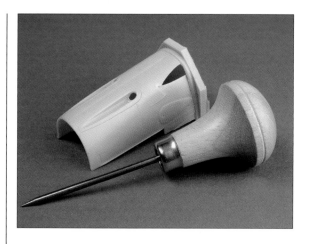

Sometimes a project does not start well. I managed to punch a large hole in Aires' Bf 109F–early G cowl while adding rivet detail. This may have been repairable, but I chose a different route.

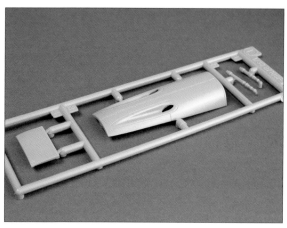

Hasegawa's Bf 109G-4 kit includes a cowl deck that will also be suitable for the G-2 variant. I used this part instead of the Aires cowling.

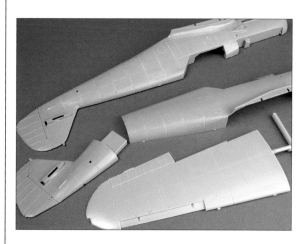

MDC's rivet-making tool was used to add further structural detail to the fuselage and wings.

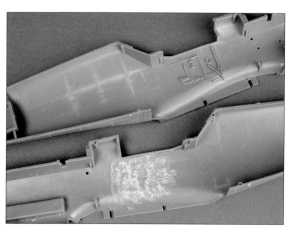

Evidence of stress placed on the plastic by the 'riveting' process is very obvious on the inside of the fuselage. Sidewall detail must be removed before installation of the aftermarket cockpit.

were built up using plastic card cut from templates. The templates were created by laying Tamiya masking tape over the kit troughs and tracing the outline onto the tape. The tape was then lifted off the kit part and onto thin plastic sheet, which was then cut to the correct shape. Although the outline was cut accurately, I left a bit of additional plastic on the inside of the rim. When each rim was glued on top of the gun troughs, the excess plastic on the inside boundary was trimmed away with a sharp knife. Sanding the inside of the gun trough blended the new rim.

Eagle Editions' replacement spinner is better shaped and detailed than Hasegawa's kit part. This resin part was prepared by drilling out a hole for the propeller shaft and for the propeller blade mounts.

The remainder of the smaller parts were now secured to the airframe, including resin elevators and rudder from Cutting Edge's 1/32-scale exterior detail set. The Cutting Edge hollowed-out exhaust stacks were used too. Before painting, a few redundant hatches needed to be filled. Milliput was once again used for this task.

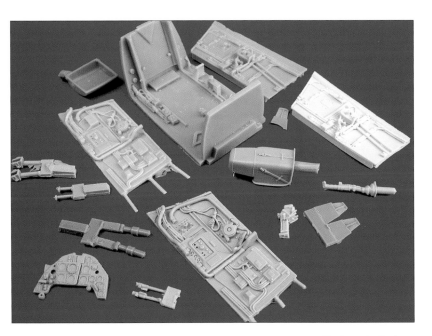

MDC offers a range of Messerschmitt Bf 109 cockpits. This is specific to the G-2, providing alternate sidewalls for the standard or tropicalized versions.

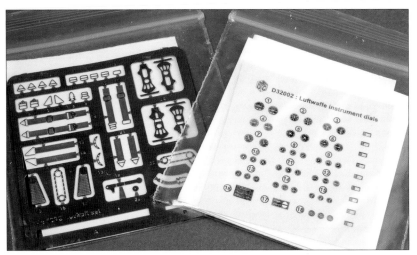

In addition to the resin parts, MDC includes decal instruments and photo-etched details.

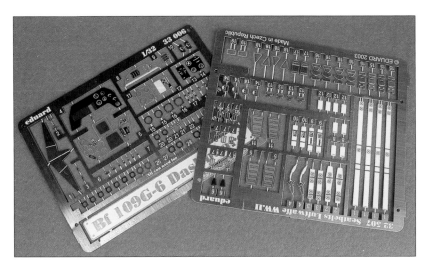

I chose to replace the MDC seat belts with Eduard's pre-painted Color-Etch harness. These look brilliant when installed. Eduard also produces a pre-painted instrument panel.

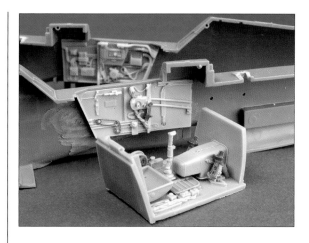

The inside of the kit fuselage halves and the back of the resin sidewalls have been thinned to improve fit. This small effort is well worthwhile.

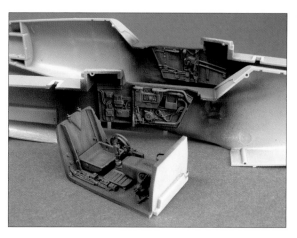

MDC's cockpit was sprayed with a base coat of Tamiya XF-1 Flat Black, followed by XF-63 German Grey. Deep structural features received a pinpoint wash of thinned oil paint. When dry, grimy streaks of black-brown were sprayed on larger surfaces.

Details such as the quadrant handles, oxygen regulator and fuel line were picked out with a fine brush. MDC's decal instruments were applied to the resin instrument panel.

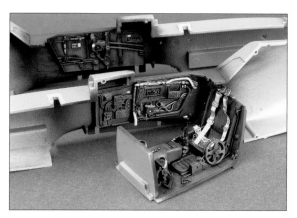

MDC includes a clear resin inspection tube for the fuel line. It is crooked in this photo but was later straightened!

Painting and markings

Finnish colours were applied over Tamiya White Surface Primer. Initially, I wanted to use a bright, moss green for Finnish Green as depicted in a number of artworks. In the end, I found it hard to justify this interpretation as all of my references pointed to a fairly drab olive green. I oversprayed my original paint job to return to reality!

I used Montex Model Club masks for the first time on the kit's canopy. These are flexible black self-adhesive vinyl masks, and they include masks for both the outside and the inside of the canopy. This is especially useful in this large scale when the canopy is open, as the internal framing is very prominent.

Markings were sourced from MDC's decal sheet D32007, 'Messerschmitt Me 109 G-2 Ilmavoimat 1943–44'. The decals performed flawlessly with the application of Micro-Set and Micro-Sol.

After a few self-induced difficulties at the beginning, this project proved to be enjoyable and quite straightforward. In my opinion, Hasegawa's 1/32-scale kits are the best Messerschmitt Bf 109s available in any scale.

Aires makes a set of replacement resin main wheel wells for Hasegawa's family of Bf 109Gs.

First, the large casting block was carefully cut off with a razor saw. The indent for the bulge in the kit upper wing halves was also covered with sheet styrene.

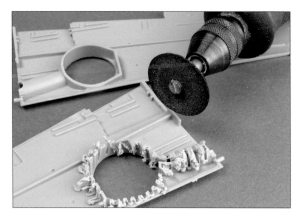

The moulded-on wheel well must also be removed. I sliced this structure with a cutting wheel fitted to a Dremel motor tool. The resulting waste was easily cleaned up with pliers and a sharp hobby knife.

Aires' wheel wells are more accurate and better detailed than the kit parts.

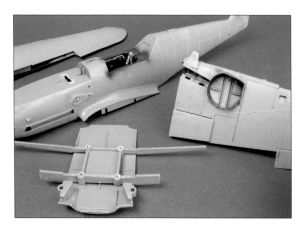

MDC's cockpit floor is thicker than the kit parts, so some height had to be trimmed off the top of the wing spar centre sections before assembly.

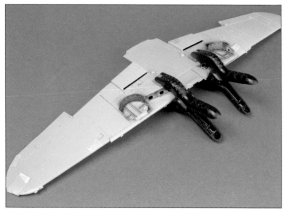

Although not the sequence recommended by the instructions, I built the entire wing before offering the assembly to the fuselage.

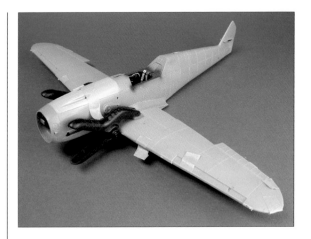

The result was a perfect, gap-free fit. Clamps were used to ensure no rogue steps appeared.

Dihedral was a little flat, so Tamiya tape provided some vertical persuasion while the liquid cement set.

The separate gun cowl results in a prominent seam line that was not on the real aircraft. Milliput was trowelled on to this panel line. Tamiya tape was used to mask off the surrounding areas.

With the tape removed, the Milliput has been restricted to a fairly narrow area. When dry, the slow-curing epoxy putty was sanded flat.

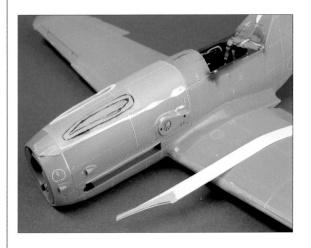

Hasegawa's gun troughs are quite flat, while the real things were separate pressings dropped into the cowl. I cut rough shapes from thin plastic strip based on a tape template.

These rough gun trough outlines were glued to the kit gun cowl.

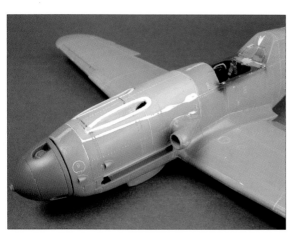

When the cement had dried, I carefully cut around the inside of the gun trough, then sanded the inside to blend the new outline with the rest of the trough.

Now it is looking like a Messerschmitt Bf 109! Basic assembly is complete, including Cutting Edge's exterior detailing set.

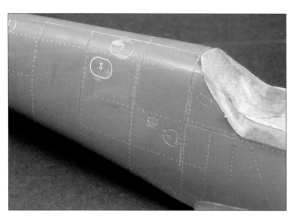

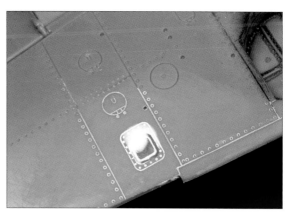

Several hatches and panel lines needed to be eliminated prior to painting.

Milliput was used to cover these engraved lines. The surrounding areas were then masked and the excess putty was sanded off.

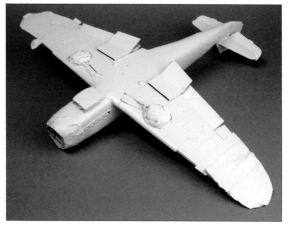

Tamiya's Fine White Primer acted both as an undercoat for the bright yellow theatre markings, and also as a useful tool to ensure there were no gaps or other surface imperfections.

The yellow theatre markings were masked and the lower surface and fuselage sides were sprayed with Tamiya AS-5 Luftwaffe Light Blue, straight from the can.

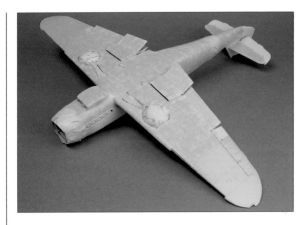

This pale colour was supplemented with a squiggly coverage of Tamiya acrylic XF-23 Light Blue. This is a much darker colour than the first coat.

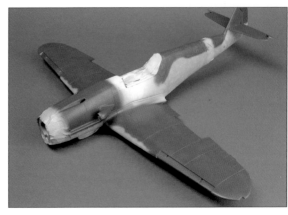

Initially I wanted to depict Finnish Olive Green as fairly light and bright. I chose Gunze H422 RLM 82 Light Green for this job.

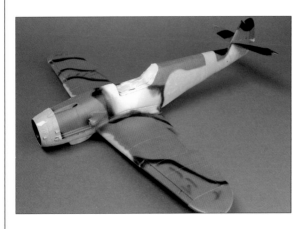

You'd think black would be pretty straightforward, but this is actually a 50:50 mix of Flat Black and RLM 70 Black Green. The outline of the disruptive pattern is sprayed first, freehand.

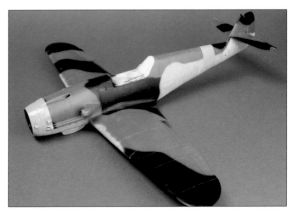

With the basic camouflage in place, it was obvious that the green was far too light and too bright.

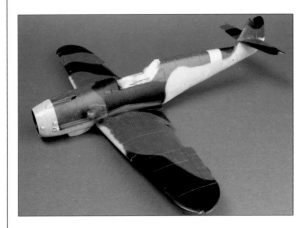

I oversprayed this light colour with something a little more subdued!

The entire airframe was coated with a messy oil wash. This was a mix of black and raw umber thinned heavily and applied by brush. Although alarming when applied, the effect can be controlled when dry.

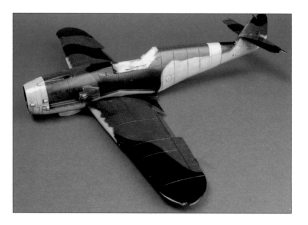

With the oil wash tamed, it was time to prepare the model for decals. A coat of Future floor polish, mixed with around 25 per cent isopropyl alcohol, provides a suitably high gloss finish.

Markings were sourced from MDC's decal sheet D32007, 'Messerschmitt Me 109G-2 Ilmavoimat 1943–44'. The decals performed flawlessly.

Montex Model Club masks were used on the canopy. The Montex set includes masks for both the outside and the inside of all canopy parts – very useful especially in this large scale.

The canopy parts have been secured with Kristal Klear, and the aerial wire has been attached to the mast. E-Z Line elastic thread was used for the aerial wire.

ABOVE Final weathering included highlighting of selected panel lines and control surface hinge lines with a thin dark mix, and the application of exhaust stains.

BELOW The kit canopy was enhanced with a canopy crank lever from scrap rod and strip, two handles for the sliding window sections punched from clear plastic, and a restraining wire.

ABOVE MDC's resin Bf 109 tail wheel was installed. This
particular aircraft was fitted with a G-6-type tail wheel, with the
faired-over lower fuselage opening.

BELOW Eagle Editions' resin spinner is a better shape and more
detailed than the kit part.

ABOVE The kit pitot tube was replaced with a filament from an industrial light.

BELOW Some 'chipping' of the paintwork along the wing root walkways was added with silver Prismacolour pencil. The tyres received light dusting with pastel chalks.

Gustav trainer

Subject:	Messerschmitt Bf 109G-12
Modeller:	Construction, painting and markings by Brett Green
Skill Level:	Master
Base Kit:	Hasegawa Bf 109G-6; Falcon vacform Bf 109G-12 conversion
Scale:	1/48
Additional detailing sets used:	Aires Bf 109G cockpit set; Cutting Edge Bf 109G cockpit set; Contact Resine spinner; plastic strip, wire and scrap pieces
Paints:	Gunze acrylics using a Testor Aztek A470 airbrush
Markings:	Various decals from the spares box, including an old War Eagle sheet

Hasegawa 1/48-scale Messerschmitt Bf 109G family
Summary
Pros
• Good level of detail
• Good fit
• Crisply recessed panel lines
• Generally accurate outlines
• Separate flaps and slats
• Thin, clear canopies
• Useful options (drop tank, cannon gondolas, alternate gun decks and canopy armour, etc.)
Cons
• Fuselage is 2mm too short (between the front of the windscreen and the back of the engine cowl)
• Spinner shape is not quite right

Falcon 1/48-scale Messerschmitt Bf 109G-12 conversion
Summary
Pros
• Accurate
• Generally good fit
• Not many other options available to build a G-12
Cons
• Significant scratch building required
• Soft surface details compared to 21st-century injection-moulded kits
• Designed for Revell 1/48-scale Bf 109G-10 (adaptation required to use with Hasegawa kits)
• Tricky vacform canopy

Introduction

Once upon a time, our hobby was not blessed with magnificently detailed resin accessories and pre-painted photo-etched enhancements. In those dark days, one of the few options available to an adventurous soul who wanted to change the shape of a model was a vacuum-formed conversion. Vacform modelling may seem to be almost irrelevant in the 21st century, but there are still some obscure yet interesting subjects that have been otherwise bypassed by the model industry.

One of these overlooked subjects is the Messerschmitt Bf 109G-12 two-seater trainer. Over the years there have been two short-lived, short-run injection-moulded and resin kits or conversions, but if you want a G-12 right now, vacform is your only option.

Falcon Industries from New Zealand produced some great vacform kits and conversions during the 1980s. Amongst these were a series of 'Triple Conversion' sets, one of which comprised conversion fuselages for a 1/48-scale Bf 109G-14, a Focke-Wulf Fw 190S-8 and a Messerschmitt Bf 109G-12. These conversions are still available today.

These conversions are simple in the extreme – basic fuselage halves plus spinners and cockpit floors and bulkheads moulded onto a thick sheet of white styrene. However, the shapes are accurate and, with some planning and patience, an impressive result is possible. Each conversion also includes a crystal clear Falcon vacform canopy.

Construction

I always find it difficult to see detail on plain white plastic, so I started by spraying the vacform sheet grey using Tamiya's Surface Primer straight from the can.

A scriber was used to score a deep line around the fuselage, after which the excess plastic sheet was simply snapped off. Sanding the parts on coarse abrasive paper eliminated the remaining thickness of the backing sheet. Enough material had been removed when the plastic was sanded to the level where the grey primer started.

Once the fuselage halves were separated from the backing sheet, the cockpit and exhaust areas were carefully opened up with a new hobby blade.

Although the canopy is not destined to be installed until the end of the project, it is essential that the width matches that of the fuselage. The canopy

The Messerschmitt Bf 109G-12 was a purpose-designed trainer version of the famous Gustav. This aircraft was attached to I./JG 104, an advanced fighter training unit.

was therefore cut from its clear backing with a sharp knife. My technique for this slightly nerve-wracking job is to pack the canopy with Blu-Tack, which adds structural rigidity to the flimsy plastic, and also makes it easier to see the cutting lines; I then use a brand-new hobby blade to score lightly around the edge of the canopy. After a few passes, the canopy will come free of its backing.

The fuselage halves were taped together and matched to the newly freed canopy. The match was generally good, but there was a wedge-shaped gap at the rear of the canopy that would need to be addressed later.

The cockpit was the next challenge. I used the rear bulkhead and the instructor's instrument panel moulded onto the vacform sheet, but all other cockpit components were sourced elsewhere. The rear canopy was adapted from resin and photo-etched parts from an Aires Bf 109G-6 cockpit, while the forward cockpit is from Cutting Edge. Both cockpits are resin with a few photo-etched details.

The rear cockpit needed some additional work before being fitted. For a start, the floor had to be cut down to fit in the narrower rear fuselage. The sidewalls also needed trimming – at the rear to suit the steeper profile of the rear bulkhead, at the bottom to cater for the shorter rear fuselage, and at the front to clear the new instrument panel and coaming. With these modifications complete, the four sidewalls were glued to the inside of the vacform fuselage prior to painting.

Both cockpits were painted using Tamiya acrylics. A base coat of XF-1 Flat Black was sprayed, followed by a light coat of XF-63 German Grey, then a thin wash of black and raw umber oil paints was applied to throw some of the high detail into relief. Coloured details were picked out with a fine brush. The forward instrument panel featured an acetate sheet with printed instruments that show through open holes in the resin panels. This is quite effective. The rear panel was detailed with instrument decals punched from a Tamiya decal sheet. The cockpit was completed with a squirt of Gunze H20 Flat Clear.

Falcon's conversion was originally designed for Revell's 1/48-scale Bf 109G-10, but Hasegawa's more recent G-6 kit is a more appropriate donor kit today. However, the parts breakdown of both kits is quite different, so some extra work is required to adapt Falcon's fuselage to Hasegawa's wings.

The lower cowl oil cooler housing was first sliced off Falcon's vacform fuselage halves, as Hasegawa's separate oil cooler is better detailed. I also installed Hasegawa's exhausts prior to joining the fuselage halves. The centre of Hasegawa's wing trailing edge was reinforced with a thick piece of styrene. This was intended to bridge a large gap between the wing and the fuselage, giving a decent bonding surface and providing a backing for filling material. The wing and fuselage assemblies were glued together with no unexpected problems. After test fitting and preparation, the fit at the upper wing root was close to perfect.

The lower fuselage needed more work. A large gap at the rear of the wing was filled with plastic sheet, while a smaller gap behind the oil cooler was packed with plastic then cut to shape. The large hole in the bottom of the cowling was backed with plastic card, which would form the roof of the oil cooler housing. After the gaps were plugged, sanded and smoothed, Hasegawa's oil cooler housing, flaps and horizontal stabilizers were glued in place.

The vacform fuselage was relatively soft in detail and devoid of structural features. Some of the more prominent panel lines and hatches were scribed onto the plastic to match the crisp recessed detail on Hasegawa's wings.

Painting and markings

With the model prepared and masked, painting proceeded conventionally.

First, the yellow markings under the engine cowl were painted with Tamiya Camel Yellow. Polly Scale acrylics were used for the camouflage colours – RLM 74 Grey Green, RLM 75 Grey Violet and RLM 76 Light Blue.

RLM 75 Grey Violet was sprayed on the upper surface after the base coat of RLM 76 Light Blue had dried. A paler shade of the grey was mixed and sprayed thinly in streaks and mottles over the RLM 75. This effect looks excessive before further painting and weathering. The camouflage pattern for the disruptive pattern of RLM 74 Grey Green was sprayed freehand. Pale streaks and mottles were also sprayed on the RLM 74 portion of the camouflage. Thin lines of RLM 74 were sprayed freehand close to the demarcation between the two upper surface colours. This subtly softened the camouflage pattern.

The irregular mottle on the forward fuselage was sprayed freehand using both RLM 74 and RLM 75, taking care to maintain the entire rear fuselage in RLM 76 Light Blue

Further consultation of the reference photo led to more work on the camouflage pattern, especially the shape and density of the mottling. This is not unusual for me. I often make significant revisions to a paint job before I am satisfied.

The reference photo indicated that the fuselage gun bulges and the rear gun cowl are painted a paler shade than the other upper surface camouflage colours. I decided that RLM 02 Grey was the most likely candidate. I masked around the bulges and rear cowl panel with Tamiya tape before spraying the area with Gunze H70 RLM 02 Grey. The wing roots were also masked, then sprayed flat black. With the basic paint job complete, the entire airframe was prepared for decals with a high gloss coat of Future floor finish.

Markings came from a number of sources. The black codes were adapted from an old War Eagle decal sheet, while the four 'White 40s' were from a couple of different armour model decal sheets. National markings and stencils came from an EagleCals decal set.

Final weathering was added in the form of thinly sprayed lines highlighting control surface hinge lines and other structural details. The same mix was used to add random streaks on the wings and fuselage. The paint job was completed with a coat of Polly Scale Flat.

Finishing touches

Without question, the most painful part of this project was the final installation of the canopy. Despite the complexities of vacform modelling and kitbashing, construction was actually quite smooth and enjoyable right up to this point. I attribute the problems partly to the euphoria of almost finishing a challenging job, thus letting my attention slip at a critical time.

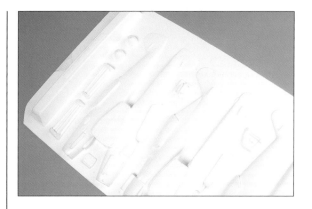

Falcon's 1/48-scale Messerschmitt Bf 109G-12 conversion is supplied on a sheet of white vacuum-formed plastic along with two other subjects – a Focke-Wulf Fw 190S and a Bf 109G-14.

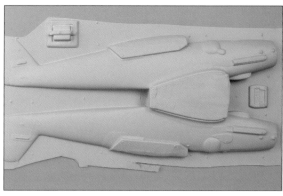

The section containing the Bf 109G-12 fuselage was cut out and sprayed with grey primer. The grey primer makes it easier to see details, and also simplifies the task of accurately removing the backing sheet.

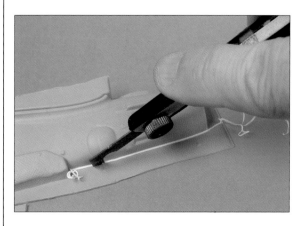

A scriber was used to score a deep line around the fuselage. After several passes, the waste material was simply snapped off.

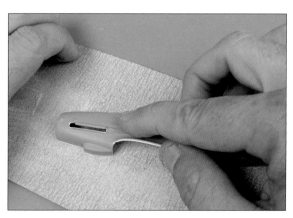

The remaining thickness of the backing sheet was eliminated by sanding the part on coarse abrasive paper. When the plastic was sanded to the level where the grey primer started, enough material had been removed.

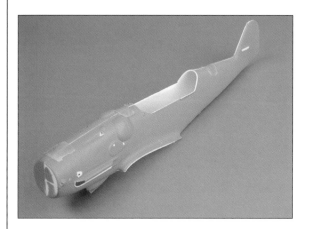

Regular test fitting is absolutely essential with such a project. Note that the space for the exhausts has been opened up here.

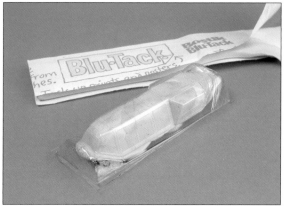

The canopy was cut out at this stage. I wanted to make sure that the width of the assembled fuselage matched the dimensions of the canopy.

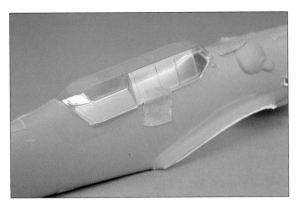

As can be seen here, the overall dimensions coincide, but there is a wedge-shaped gap at the rear of the canopy.

Falcon supplies a basic floor and rear bulkhead, but all other cockpit details must be sourced elsewhere. The rear canopy was adapted from resin and photo-etched parts from an Aires Bf 109G-6 cockpit, while the forward cockpit is from Cutting Edge.

Cockpit sidewalls were glued to the inside of the fuselage, and the parts were ready for painting.

With so many small cockpit subassemblies, I kept track by attaching the parts to a small box during painting. I was also painting the Airfix Bf 109F cockpit and a 1/48-scale Focke-Wulf Fw 190A-8 cockpit at the same time!

The painted tandem cockpit looks suitably busy. Falcon supplies the rear instrument panel as two vacform parts.

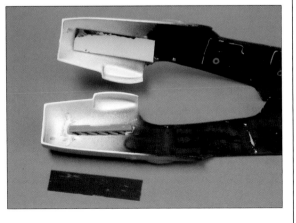

Exhausts from Hasegawa's 1/48-scale Bf 109G-6 were adapted for installation. When the parts were glued in place they were backed with plastic sheet to blank off any gaps.

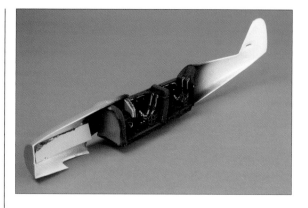

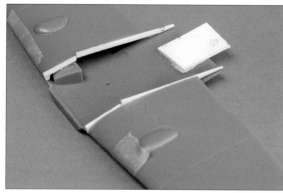

All the custom-built cockpit parts fitted into the fuselage without any problems.

Test fitting suggested that the fuselage might be too wide at the wing root, so I shaved a little more than 1mm from the inside of each top wing half. Final fitting disproved that theory, so I had to return the wings to their original dimensions with plastic shims.

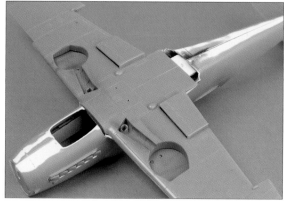

The fit of the fuselage halves, the wings and the tailplanes was good thanks to plenty of planning and test fitting.

The situation underneath required some more attention. The conversion was designed for the Revell Bf 109G-10, resulting in some large but not unexpected gaps.

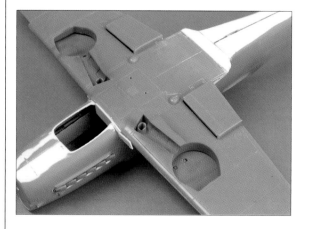

The large gap at the trailing edge of the wing was addressed with a piece of plastic strip cut to shape and blended in with putty. The smaller gap at the front of the wing was plugged with styrene card.

The lower nose was adapted to accept Hasegawa's oil cooler housing. The roof of the oil cooler area was blanked off with plastic card.

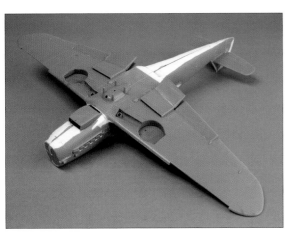

Hasegawa's oil cooler housing was a big improvement over the vacuum-formed part originally moulded to the fuselage halves.

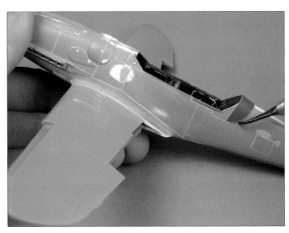

The vacform fuselage was relatively soft in detail and devoid of structural features. Some of the more prominent panel lines and hatches were scribed onto the plastic.

There are several areas where panel lines have been erased and rescribed, as can be seen where the grey primer has been sanded off. At this stage, the model is almost ready for paint.

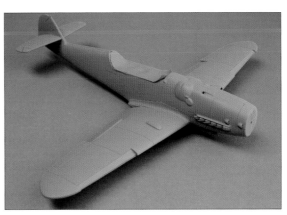

Another coat of grey primer, this time over the entire airframe, helps identify any remaining imperfections.

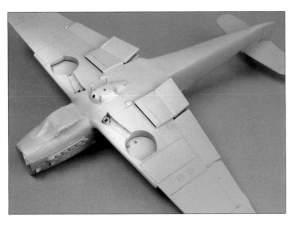

The lower cowl was first painted yellow over a white undercoat. This area was masked off with Tamiya tape when the yellow paint had completely dried.

Next, the model received a coat of Polly Scale acrylic RLM 76 Light Blue on the lower surfaces and the entire fuselage.

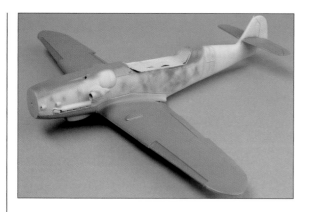

Polly Scale RLM 75 Grey Violet followed. I was careful to keep the rear fuselage free of the darker camouflage colours.

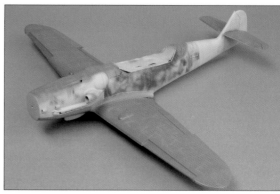

The basic grey was disrupted with a random application of a lighter shade. The fuselage mottle was built up with Polly Scale RLM 74 Grey Green.

The wings were also painted in this second camouflage colour, and more work was applied to the fuselage mottle using a reference photo as a guide.

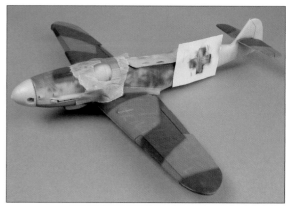

The cannon bulges seemed to be painted a lighter colour according to the reference photo. The bulges and the associated panel were masked and sprayed Gunze H70 RLM 02 Grey. A custom mask was also used to isolate a darker pattern inside the fuselage cross.

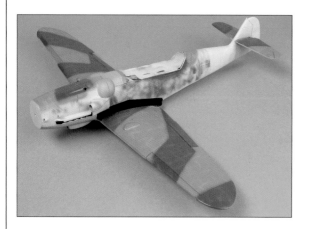

Detail painting took place now, including the black wing root and the metallic exhaust stubs.

Following a coat of Polly Scale Gloss, the decals were applied. These were scrounged from a number of sources, including an old War Eagle sheet.

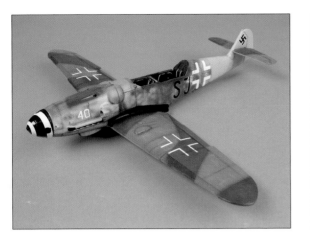

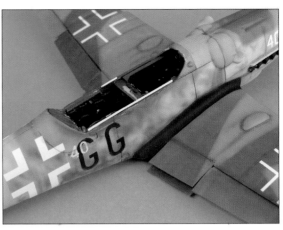

With the decals in place, it was time for some additional weathering of panel lines and control surfaces.

A narrow ridge of plastic strip was glued to the rim of the cockpit to provide a solid join for the thin vacform canopy.

I prepared the model for the installation of the canopy by gluing thin strips of plastic along the cockpit sill. These strips would provide a positive locating point for the thin vacform plastic, and a convenient spot to apply glue. I test fitted and all appeared well but, after applying watchmaker's glue to the cockpit rim, I could not get the canopy to line up without noticeable gaps. In the end, I had to pull the canopy off the model and try to clean the sticky mess off the top of the fuselage sides. For my second attempt I used Micro Kristal Klear as the adhesive. I figured that, if I still had gaps, I could at least use the Kristal Klear as filler. In the end, that is what happened. Gaps underneath each side of the windscreen and at the back of the rear canopy were filled with Kristal Klear, and then brush painted to roughly blend in with the surrounding camouflage. The result is still not entirely pretty. If Falcon provided a second vacform canopy with the conversion I would have certainly started over.

Mercifully, the remaining details were assembled without hassle. The drop tank, undercarriage legs, wheels and propeller assembly were glued in place and the model was complete.

The canopy was masked with Tamiya tape. The multiple frames make this a tedious task (I suppose I should be thankful that I am not building a Junkers Ju 188).

ABOVE The spinner and propeller blades are from French accessory company Contact Resine.

BELOW The canopy did not fit terribly well, requiring ample amounts of Kristal Klear to fair in multiple small gaps and steps.

Conclusion

I think that the Messerschmitt Bf 109G-12 is a very appealing aircraft. With luck, we might have a 1/48- or 1/32-scale injection-moulded option in the future.

In the meantime though, Falcon's Bf 109G-12 conversion might be an interesting and challenging project for a modeller who would like to make their first attempt at vacform.

ABOVE Teknics' resin drop tank was installed, as were True Details' wheels. Navigation lights were painted onto each wingtip using transparent red and green.

BELOW The tandem cockpits deliver a very different profile to the otherwise familiar lines of the Messerschmitt Bf 109G.

Wilde Sau

Subject:	Messerschmitt Bf 109G-14
Modeller:	Construction, painting and markings by Brett Green
Skill Level:	Advanced
Base Kit:	Hobbycraft Bf 109G-14
Scale:	1/48
Additional detailing sets used:	Cooper Details' cockpit; windscreen, Erla Haube canopy, supercharger intake, gun deck and cannon bulges from Hasegawa's Bf 109G-14 kit; Eagle Editions' spinner; various plastic and metal strip, sheet and scrap
Paints:	Gunze and Tamiya acrylics applied with the Testor Aztek metal-bodied airbrush
Markings:	Various decals from Aeromaster's 48-001 and several EagleCals sheets

Hobbycraft's 1/48-scale Messerschmitt Bf 109F and G family

Summary

Pros

• Accurate outlines and dimensions
• Recessed panel lines
• Good fit
• Many options including drop tank, bomb racks and tropical filter
• Nice, three-piece tail wheel assembly
• Available inexpensively

Cons

• Poorly shaped detail parts including spinner, gun deck, supercharger intake and breech bulges
• No option for dropped slats or flaps
• Undersized windscreen and thick canopy
• Inconsistent panel lines (some are very shallow)
• Indifferent cockpit detail

Construction

Hobbycraft's 1/48-scale Messerschmitt Bf 109F and G kits are accurate in overall dimensions and outline, and they may be purchased inexpensively. Academy has more recently re-released these kits under their own label with much improved decals too. However, in almost every other respect, Hobbycraft's Friedrichs and Gustavs lag significantly behind Hasegawa's equivalents.

When I finished building my Messerschmitt Bf 109G-12, I had a large number of Hasegawa parts left over from the project, including the canopy, gun cowl and fuselage breech bulges. Many of these parts coincided with the weaker aspects of Hobbycraft's kit. I wondered if Hasegawa's superior detail parts could be adapted to fit Hobbycraft's fuselage which was, after all, dimensionally more accurate than Hasegawa's. There was only one way to find out!

Comparison of the cowl deck and the windscreen with Hobbycraft's fuselage indicated that surgery would be required. I prepared the fuselage by carefully extending the opening in the top of Hobbycraft's nose to the length of the Hasegawa gun cowl insert. I also cut out the triangular area immediately below the windscreen on each side of the Hobbycraft fuselage. Test fitting suggested that the windscreen would be a good fit, but that more work was required to blend the Hasegawa cowl deck with the Hobbycraft nose. This would wait until later.

Hobbycraft's cockpit is quite basic so I decided to replace it with the excellent resin set from Cooper Details. Cooper Details was one of the pioneers of resin detail sets in the late 1980s, and this set still compares well with today's state of the art. A nice bonus is the inclusion of a set of hollowed-out resin exhausts and a white-metal tail wheel assembly. Although the Cooper Details cockpit was originally designed for the contemporary Revell 1/48-scale Bf 109G-10, it fits the Hobbycraft G-6/14 quite well.

The kit's fuselage sidewalls were thinned by repeatedly grazing a cutting wheel fitted to a Dremel motor tool along the plastic surface. Coarse sandpaper was used to knock off some of the rough edges before the Cooper Details sidewalls were glued to the inside of the fuselage.

Attention was now returned to the gun cowl. The Hasegawa part rode high on the nose, and the rear cross section profile was squarer than the Hobbycraft

fuselage. I therefore cut a very fine wedge from each side of the fuselage immediately below the gun deck. This significantly improved the fit.

The remainder of the resin cockpit was assembled without problems, and then painted using Tamiya acrylics. A thin wash of black and raw umber oil paints was applied to suggest depth and shadows. Some fine vertical streaks in Tamiya XF-24 Dark Grey were applied with the airbrush to add some irregularity to the paint finish before coloured details were picked out with a fine brush. Cockpit placard decals from Reheat were also added to likely locations around the cockpit before a final flat coat sealed the paint job.

The fuselage halves were now joined and the real work in blending the new cowl deck began. Hasegawa's cowl deck was secured in place with Tamiya extra-thin liquid cement. There were no gaps evident, but there was a noticeable horizontal recessed seam where the parts joined. There was also a step between the fuselage halves at the front of the nose. Both these problems were dealt with using Milliput. The two-part epoxy putty was trowelled onto the offending areas and left to dry overnight. Once set, the Milliput was sanded smooth, eliminating the unsightly step and seam lines.

At this stage I also added a door for the pilot's stowage compartment to the rear of the canopy. The door was cut from thin scrap styrene, and the hinge was a simple length of brass wire.

Unlike Hasegawa's Bf 109s, Hobbycraft's wings do not feature positionable slats or flaps. The only area requiring attention was the roof of the wheel well. I was not planning to spend too much time on this area, but I did fill the exposed locating holes for the upper wing bulges and added two strips of styrene to each wheel well as structural detail.

This Messerschmitt Bf 109G-14 wears an interesting combination of hybrid markings – the 'Pik As' (Ace of Spades) emblem of JG 53 and the broad red RV band of JG 300.

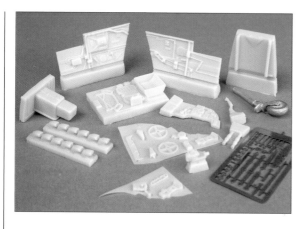

Cooper Details' 1/48-scale Messerschmitt Bf 109G cockpit predates most other resin detail sets, but remains a high-quality option. This cockpit is now marketed by Hawkeye Designs.

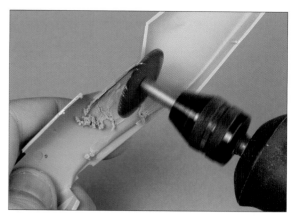

The fuselage interior needs to be thinned to accommodate the new resin cockpit sidewalls. A cutting wheel is grazed along the surface to gradually remove plastic.

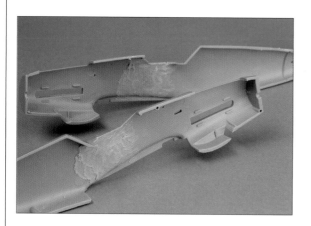

The fuselage interior is now ready to receive the resin parts.

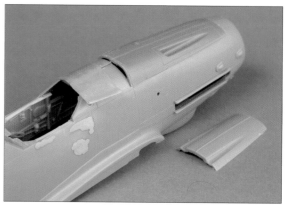

Hobbycraft's 1/48-scale Messerschmitt Bf 109F and G kits are let down by the details. Hasegawa's cowl deck is more accurate, but modifications are required for its installation.

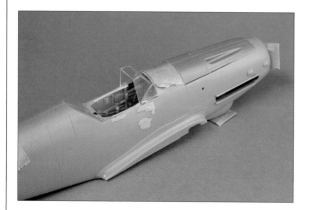

Hobbycraft's poor windscreen was replaced with Hasegawa's canopy parts. A section of the mid fuselage immediately under the windscreen was cut away to make way for the Hasegawa part. The forward fuselage has been modified to improve the fit of the Hasegawa cowl deck.

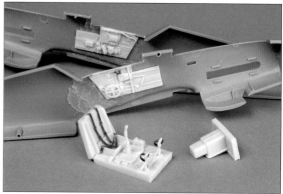

Cooper Details' cockpit was originally designed for Revell's 1/48-scale Messerschmitt Bf 109G-10, but it fits the Hobbycraft kit quite well. The sidewalls have been glued to the fuselage interior prior to painting.

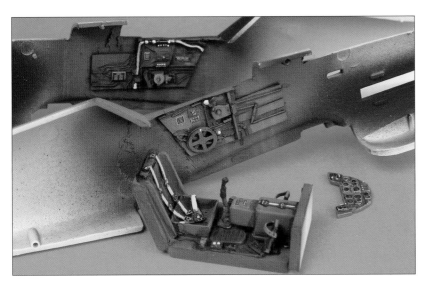

This older resin cockpit responds well to a careful paint job. Cockpit placard decals from Reheat add authenticity to the interior.

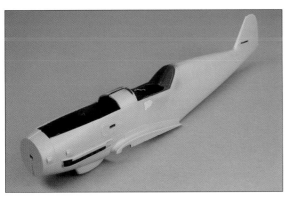

The opening for the cowl deck has been extended back to make way for the longer Hasegawa part. Cooper Details' resin exhaust stacks have also been fitted.

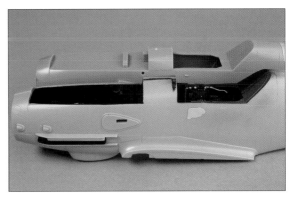

The Hasegawa Bf 109F and G kits (rear) are superior to Hobbycraft's counterparts in almost every other respect, but the Hobbycraft fuselage length is actually more accurate. Hasegawa's forward fuselage is around four scale inches short between the front of the windscreen and the rear of the engine cowl. The difference can be seen in this photo.

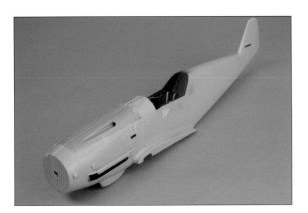

The gun deck is glued in place, but the obvious seam line still needs to be eliminated.

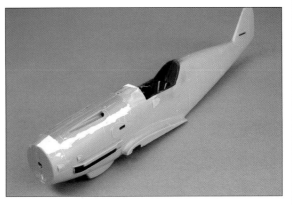

The seam between the deck and the side of the cowl, plus a step on the extreme front of the nose, were dealt with using Milliput two-part epoxy putty.

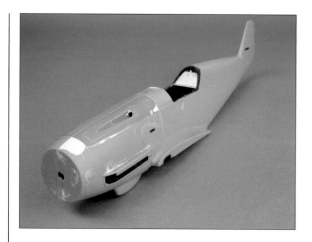

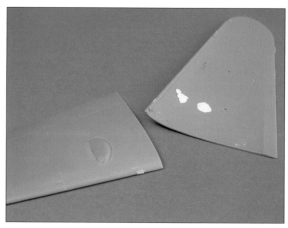

The putty was sanded and polished to obtain a smooth finish. A door for the pilot's stowage bin has been fashioned from styrene sheet, with a hinge from brass wire.

Hobbycraft's wings do not feature separate flaps and slats. Locating holes for the upper wing bulges will be visible inside the wheel wells, so these are filled with putty.

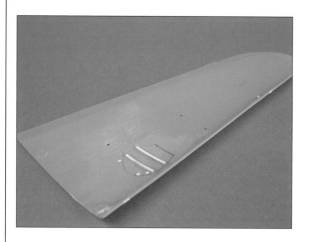

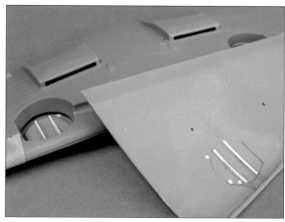

Some minor structural detail was also added on the roof of the wheel well in the form of two strips of plastic.

The result is a basic, but tidier, wheel well.

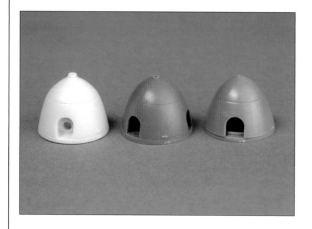

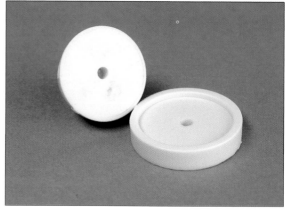

The shape of Hobbycraft's spinner, to the right of this photo, is not entirely accurate. Hasegawa's spinner (centre) is better but Eagle Editions' resin part is noticeably more accurate than both.

Eagle Editions' spinner includes a clever resin jig to drill a centred hole in the baseplate.

The shape of Hobbycraft's spinner is poor, so this was replaced with the much more accurate resin item from Eagle Editions. I particularly liked the jig supplied with Eagle Editions' spinner to permit the drilling of an accurately centred hole for the propeller shaft.

As can be seen in the comparison photos, Hobbycraft's supercharger intake and cowl gun bulges are also incorrectly shaped. Hasegawa's counterparts were glued into place with only a little filler required at the back of the bulges.

With the wings and the fuselage subassemblies complete, it was time to see how they would fit together. Initial test fitting revealed that there would be a gap at each wing root, so the fuselage was widened using a spreader bar. This bar was simply a piece of sprue cut to the appropriate size.

Once the wings were glued in place the dihedral looked a little flat. A couple of degrees were added by running Tamiya tape from wingtip to wingtip while the glue dried.

Painting and markings

I have been looking for an excuse to paint a Hungarian Bf 109 scheme, and this seemed to be the perfect opportunity. I had an old Aviation USK decal sheet with an interesting Hungarian option. I also had a photograph of the decal subject, which seemed to suggest that it was at least partially finished in late-war colours. Using the Messerschmitt Bf 109G-6 in the Australian War Memorial as a partial guide to these colours, I set to work.

After spraying and masking the yellow theatre markings, the remainder of the cowl, the bottom of the wings and the rudder were painted Gunze acrylic H417 RLM 76. The fuselage aft of the engine cowl was painted Tamiya XF-21 Sky, representing one of the late-war Luftwaffe green-blue shades. The engine cowling seemed to be finished in different colours to the rest of the fuselage, so I painted the top of the cowl deck in RLM 74 Grey Green and RLM 75 Grey Violet. The fuselage spine was masked in order to spray a relatively hard-edged, scalloped camouflage demarcation. The colours used for the spine were Gunze H304 Olive Drab representing RLM 81 Brown Violet, and Gunze H423 RLM 83 Dark Green. The fuselage side was also mottled in these colours. The tops of the wings and tailplanes were painted using Gunze H69 RLM 75 Grey Violet and H423 RLM 83 Dark Green, with a patch of RLM 81 close to the port side wing root.

With the intricate paint job out of the way it was time for decals. The entire Aviation USK sheet was covered with decal film, so the individual markings were cut out. The decal film was quite thick, so I decided to use only the unique markings from the Aviation USK sheet. The Hungarian national markings were sourced from Aeromaster decals very first release, 48-001. These Hungarian markings had a white interior though, so I masked and sprayed the inside of the fuselage and upper wing crosses RLM 83 Dark Green. The *Werknummer* and aircraft codes were reluctant to settle into panel lines. I only obtained a reasonable result after slicing the decals with a new hobby blade and applying several coats of Micro-Sol. The Aeromaster decals performed well though.

The painted and decaled model now received a wash of heavily thinned oil paint. I mixed lamp black and raw umber 50:50, and thinned it to a watery consistency with odourless thinners.

Sometimes, despite the best intentions, a paint job simply does not meet expectations. I just did not like the way the model looked. To my eye, the scheme did not look authentic and the execution was not pleasing in a number of areas, especially the overspray from the fuselage mottle, the too-hard camouflage demarcation on the spine and the too-soft demarcation on the wings. After setting the model aside for two months I finally decided to start over.

The decals were stripped off. Packing tape was used to remove large sections of the decal, while the less cooperative remnants were sanded off with 100-grit Tamiya abrasive paper. The entire model was then lightly sanded with 100-grit

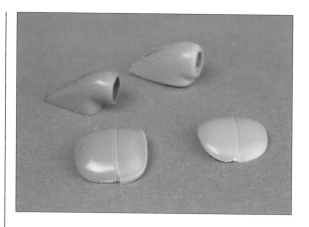

Hasegawa's supercharger intake and cannon breech bulges are vastly superior to Hobbycraft's misshapen equivalents. Hasegawa's parts were used for this project.

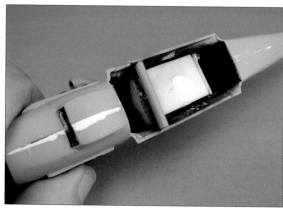

Test fitting suggested that there would be a gap at the wing root, so the fuselage was widened with a spreader bar cut from plastic sprue.

The spreader bar ensured a gap-free fit between the wings and the fuselage. Dihedral was set using Tamiya tape stretched from wingtip to wingtip.

With the canopy masked off, painting commenced with yellow theatre markings and a coat of Gunze H417 RLM 76 on the fuselage.

This late-war scheme comprised a patchwork of colours. Next was Tamiya XF-21 RAF Sky, representing one of the Luftwaffe shades used in the final months of the war.

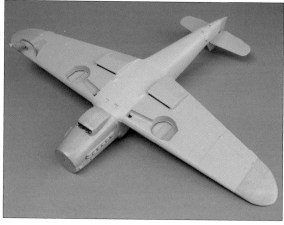

It was not uncommon to see two or more different colours used on the lower surface of Luftwaffe fighters at this chaotic stage.

The nose was finished in a fairly conventional scheme of RLM 74 Grey Green and RLM 75 Grey Violet, but the mid and rear fuselage was another story. Post-It Notes were used to mask a scalloped demarcation along the fuselage sides.

RLM 81 Brown Violet was next. This is an unstable colour that can appear to be dark green, red brown or even a faded olive drab. For this model I chose an olive drab incarnation.

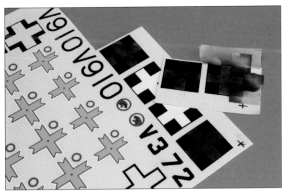

The main disruptive colour was RLM 83 Dark Green (Gunze H423). The yellow chevron poking around from under the port wing is a southern theatre marking.

Markings for a late-war Hungarian Messerschmitt Bf 109G-14 were sourced from Aeromaster's very first decal sheet – 48-001. Although old, the decals performed well. The white interior of the fuselage and upper wing crosses were filled with RLM 83 Dark Green.

The scheme is taking shape. The colours were based on the scheme applied to a similar Bf 109G-6 in the Australian War Memorial, and on the interpretation of a poor-quality black and white photo.

The chevron and the Hungarian markings combine to make an interesting subject.

As interesting as the subject might have been in theory though, I was not happy with my execution. The model was shelved for months while I decided how to improve the result.

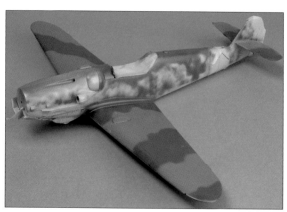

One afternoon I picked up the model, stripped off the decals and polished the model back to a smooth finish. Sometimes, starting over is the best option.

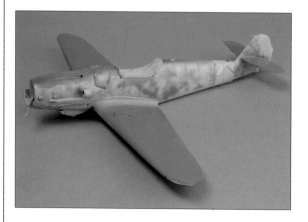

Unlike the first angst-ridden and time-consuming attempt, this paint job was almost effortless. The yellow markings on the cowl and wingtips were masked, and the fuselage was resprayed with RLM 76 Light Blue. Here is the first pass of RLM 75 Grey Violet.

And here is the first coat of RLM 74 Grey Green, with the heavy fuselage mottle starting to take shape.

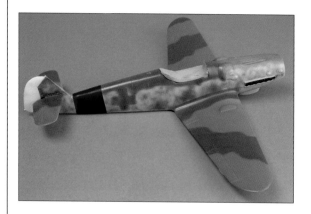

The dull red fuselage band is the unmistakable marking of a JG 300 'Wilde Sau'. The new paint job, from the beginning of masking until this point, took less than three hours.

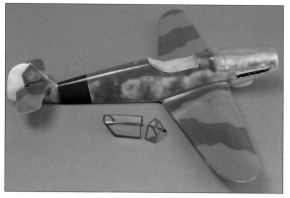

The following day, the model was sprayed with an overall coat of Future floor polish, thinned with isopropyl alcohol. I find that the alcohol speeds the drying time and inhibits the thick runs sometimes encountered when spraying undiluted Future.

ABOVE I based this scheme on a photo in the Jadgwaffe book *Defending the Reich 1944–1945*. The aircraft is described as having a black RV band, but it seems much lighter than that. A number of JG 53 aircraft were loaned to JG 300 in 1943 and 1944. This may have been one of them.

BELOW The fuselage number was a unique style. I could not find any decals to match, so I modified a 'Red 13' from an old Aeromaster sheet. The other decals were all raided from Eagle Editions' decal sheets.

ABOVE Hobbycraft's tail wheel is actually quite nice, coming as three separate pieces that can be displayed castered off-centre. The DF loop was bent from a staple, while the aerial wire is elastic EZ-Line.

BELOW Hobbycraft's drop tank was detailed with a breather tube in the front and feeder pipes in the top, all from fine wire.

paper, followed by polishing with progressively finer grades of Micro-Mesh polishing cloth. The old scheme could still be seen, but the surface of the model was smooth enough for the new paint job.

Unlike the problematic initial scheme, the new paint job was a breeze. In less than three hours I had the basic colours in place.

Decals were pilfered from a number of sources including 'Red 13' from Aeromaster 48-003, and national markings from an Eagle Editions sheet.

Exhaust staining was added to the fuselage side using a very thin mix of Tamiya XF-1 Flat Black and XF-64 Red Brown, plus a small blob of X-21 Flat Base. This broad streak was followed by a thinner, darker exhaust line.

Fuse wire was used for hydraulic lines on the front of the undercarriage legs, strapped in place with fine lengths of Tamiya masking tape.

Selected panel lines and random dirty streaks were added from the thin black and red-brown mix. The final flat coat was Polly Scale Flat acrylic.

Conclusion

There is no doubt that Hasegawa's 1/48-scale Bf 109G kits are superior to their Hobbycraft counterparts in most respects. However, Hobbycraft's basic airframe is decent, and the fuselage dimensions are actually better than Hasegawa's. With the substitution of Hasegawa's canopy, cannon bulges, cowl deck and supercharger intake, Hobbycraft's Bf 109G-14 looks pretty good.

If you have Hobbycraft's kit and various spares from a Hasegawa Gustav lying around, this might be a worthwhile project!

ABOVE Not surprisingly, Hasegawa's Erla Haube canopy is very nice – thin and almost completely free of distortion. The isolator and tension spring on the aerial wire were formed from Kristal Klear.

BELOW Hobbycraft's 1/48-scale Messerschmitt Bf 109G-6/14 kit runs a distant second place to Hasegawa but, with work (and a lot of parts from the spares box), it can be lifted to a reasonable standard.

Further reading and websites

Selected Bf 109F and G references

List compiled by Charles Metz

Abe, K., Yokoyama, K., and Kano, S., *Messerschmitt Bf 109G-6* (Modeler's Eye series, No. 3; Dai-Nippon Kaiga, Tokyo, 2002; in Japanese and English; 88 pages)

Beaman, J., *Last of the Eagles* (privately published, Greensboro, NC, 1976; 95 pages)

Beaman, J., *Messerschmitt Bf 109 in Action (Part 2)* (Aircraft in Action series, No. 57; Squadron/Signal, Carrollton, TX, 1983)

Fernandez-Sommerau, M., *Messerschmitt Bf 109 Recognition Manual* (Classic Publications, Hersham, UK, 2004; 224 pages)

Green, B., *Augsburg's Last Eagles: Colors, Markings and Variants* (Eagle Files series, No. 3; Eagle Editions, Hamilton, MT, 2000; 80 pages)

Griehl, M., *Messerschmitt Bf 109F* (Luftwaffe Profile series, Nos. 13; Schiffer, Atglen, PA, 1999; 49 pages)

Griehl, M., *Messerschmitt Bf-109G/K* (Flugzeug Profile series, No. 5; Flugzeug Publikations, Illertissen, Germany, undated; in German and English; 48 pages)

Ledwoch, J., *Bf 109F* (Wydawnictwo Militaria series, No. 54; Wydawnictwo 'Militaria', Warsaw, 1997; in Polish; 54 pages)

Ledwoch, J., *Bf 109G/H* (Wydawnictwo Militaria series, No. 47; Wydawnictwo 'Militaria', Warsaw, 1997; in Polish; 106 pages)

Merrick, K., *German Aircraft Interiors 1935–1945: Vol. 1* (Monogram Aviation Publications, Sturbridge, MA, 1996; 256 pages)

Messerschmitt Bf 109 (Maru Mechanic series, No. 39; Kojinsha, Japan, 1983; in Japanese; 80 pages)

Messerschmitt Bf 109F (Model Art Special Issue series, No. 408; Model Art, Tokyo, 1993; in Japanese; 168 pages)

Messerschmitt Bf 109G in Detail (Militaria in Detail series, No. 5; Wydawnictwo 'Militaria', Warsaw, 2000; in English; 62 pages)

Messerschmitt Bf 109G/K Augsburg Eagle (Model Art Special Issue series, No. 290; Model Art, Tokyo, 1987; in Japanese; 178 pages)

Michulec, R., *Messerschmitt Me 109, pt. 2* (Aircraft Monograph series, No. 17; AJ Press, Gdansk, 2002; in English; 121 pages)

Michulec, R., *Messerschmitt Me 109, pt. 3* (Aircraft Monograph series, No. 18; AJ Press, Gdansk, 2002; in English; 121 pages)

Nohara, S., and Shiwaku, M., *Messerschmitt Bf 109G* (Aero Detail series, No. 5; Dai-Nippon Kaiga, Tokyo, 1992; in Japanese and English; 100 pages)

Peczkowski, R., *Messerschmitt Bf 109G* (Mushroom Model Magazine Special series, No. 6112; Mushroom Model Publications, Redbourne, UK, 2004; 120 pages)

Prien, J., and Rodeike, P., *Messerschmitt Bf 109F, G, & K Series* (Schiffer, Atglen, PA, 1993; 208 pages)

Radinger, W., and Otto, W., *Messerschmitt Bf 109F-K* (Schiffer, Atglen, PA, 1999; 158 pages)

Verlinden, F., and Letterman, R., *Messerschmitt Bf 109G-2* (Lock On Aircraft Photo File series, No. 28; Verlinden Publications, O'Fallon, MO, 1997; 47 pages)

Vogt, H., *Messerschmitt Bf 109G/K Rüstsätze* (Flugzeug Profile series, No. 21; Flugzeug Publikations, Illertissen, Germany, undated; in German; 56 pages)

Websites with Messerschmitt Bf 109 content

The 109 Lair http://www.109lair.com

Falcon's Messerschmitt Hangar http://www.messerschmitt-bf109.de/index-1024.php

Le Messerschmitt 109 http://www.messerschmitt109.com/

HyperScale http://www.hyperscale.com

Scale-model-related website including articles and galleries on the Bf 109 in all scales

Modeling Madness http://www.modelingmadness.com

Aircraft Resource Center http://www.aircraftresourcecenter.com

Internet Modeler http://www.internetmodeler.com

Armorama http://www.armorama.com

Index

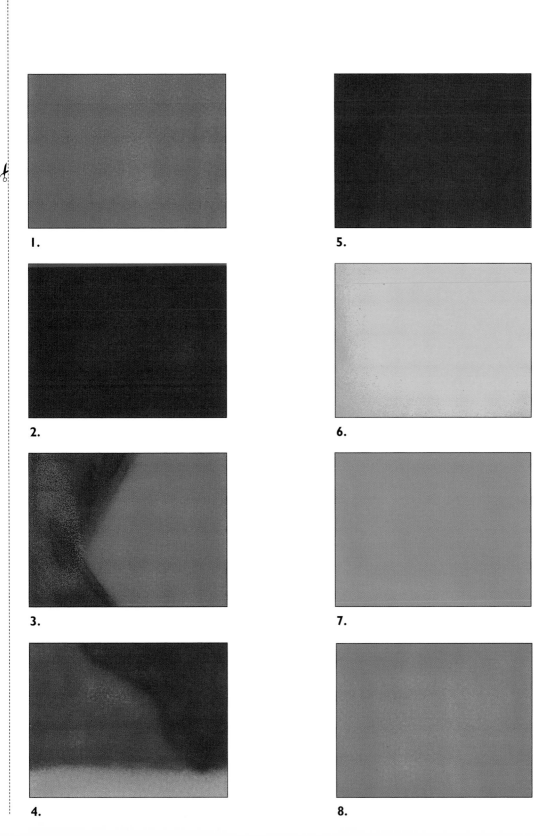

1.

2.

3.

4.

5.

6.

7.

8.

5.

In late 1944, new fighter camouflage colours were introduced. These included RLM 81 Brown Violet and RLM 83 Dark Green.

1.

RLM 02 Grey was used as an interior throughout the war, and a disruptive camouflage colour on some Eastern Front Bf 109Fs and Gs in the early stages of Operation *Barbarossa*.

6.

RLM 04 Yellow was frequently used on engine cowls, rudders and wing tips as a quick identification colour.

2.

RLM 66 Dark Grey was the standard cockpit colour for the Bf 109F and G, although other interior surfaces retained their RLM 02 finish.

7.

In the final months of the war some new, undocumented colours appeared on the lower surfaces of Luftwaffe fighters. This is a sample of one of those 'Sky' shades.

3.

It is possible that the earliest Bf 109F-0s may have worn the Battle of Britain scheme of RLM 02 Grey and RLM 71 Dark Green, or possibly mixed greys. This is a sample of 02 and 71.

8.

A small number of high altitude and 'night harassment' Bf 109s wore an overall coat of RLM 76 Light Blue.

4.

The vast majority of Messerschmitt Bf 109Fs and Gs wore the mid-war day-fighter scheme of RLM 74 Grey Green and RLM 75 Grey Violet over RLM 76 Light Blue.